Incest to Where?

by
Ruth Toby

authorHOUSE™

1663 LIBERTY DRIVE, SUITE 200
BLOOMINGTON, INDIANA 47403
(800) 839-8640
WWW.AUTHORHOUSE.COM

First published by AuthorHouse 01/31/2006

ISBN: 1-4208-3376-6 (sc)

Printed in the United States of America
Bloomington, Indiana

This book is printed on acid-free paper.

TABLE OF CONTENTS

CHAPTER ONE

I

I cannot remember what time of day or night it was except for the fact that the room was in partial darkness. There were no windows, and the only rays of light that filtered into the ramshackle room came from the adjoining door that led to my grandfather's room.

I remember I was lying on a bed, my mind blank and devoid of all thoughts. Such was the state of my life at that time. I lived mechanically, like a mindless machine.

I didn't hear any footsteps or the sound of the door opening, but suddenly I could sense the presence of someone in the room. My eyes were accustomed to seeing in the dark from being shut away frequently in my room.

They wandered around the room like a pair of search lights until they stopped on a dark figure leaning against the wall.

Perhaps aware of the fact of being seen, the figure moved slightly away from the wall. Silhouetted on the wall and part of the ceiling was a larger-than-life, averagely built figure that stood before me.

Slowly, the figure began to move toward me. I was neither frightened nor apprehensive. I lived in a little world of my own where fear did not exist. My heart was thumping in innocence, which is its natural state.

Halfway between the wall and the bed I was laying on, the rays of light that came from the door shone on the figure revealing a man naked from his waist downwards. I could not see his face. His penis was erect in front of him, and slowly, as he crouched down toward me, I saw a face which turned into a network of obscene gestures as he contorted his face muscles. I stared at this nightmarish figure with the detachment of one looking at a spectacle that had long lost its novelty. But it was a spectacle I had never seen before. The man stretched out both hands and made contact with me. The blankets I had tucked myself into for comfort were ripped away. I lay naked on the bed. Helpless and momentarily stupefied, I found my wrists held very hard in his clenched fist. His hands were trembling; they were moist and cold. Effortlessly, he turned me over on my tummy. For the first time, a wave of fear rippled through my body. I had no idea what was going to happen to me.

Suddenly, I felt suffocated as he leaned his weight on me. I felt I was carrying the entire world on my back. Something hard and hot parted the cheeks of my buttocks. It was his penis. Like a piston being thrust into a mortar, he jerked himself violently in and out of me, panting like a spent runner. Each time he thrust his penis into my backside, a

3

burning sensation went through me like acid. I screamed in pain but not for long. Steel-like hands covered my mouth, choking any sounds I tried to make.

After what seemed an eternity, during which time I felt life was being squeezed out of me, the man rolled away from me. The old, dirty blankets were stained with the blood and excrement that came from me. His desires and passions satisfied, he left the room quickly. The man was Shalom Toby, my father, and I was Ruth Toby, his three-year-old daughter. An incestuous, sexual orgy forced upon me by a degenerate member of the human race, who happened to be my father, was my very first introduction to him, the first memory I ever had, the first picture I saw as a very little girl. It was a way of telling me, "Hello, I am your father, how do you do?" A memory I will probably take to my grave. Anything that happened to me before then was buried beyond recall in my subconscious mind. My juvenile mind could not discriminate between good and bad objectively; I didn't know that something immoral had happened to me. I had been polluted and adulterated and did not know it for a long time.

So, amidst the filth around me, when I sank my face into my pillow it was not to cry but to return to my mindless existence.

II

If by destiny you mean the purposeful end or fate of a person's existence is appointed and unavoidable, I do not wholly believe in it.

I do not believe my life's journey had been mapped out by some divine or supreme being, and I had been thrown on life's perilous road to embark on and complete the journey. If I did, I would believe I was created a fly in the universal ointment. A girl created for small things, to be hated, oppressed, ridiculed, and tormented.

Some people tell me I'm too sensitive and emotional, that I am a crank and a funny person. That is their privilege. They do not know, and will never know, what makes me tick as a person.

They also say I have no education. *What is education*? I often ask myself. My concept of education is what I have learned from experience. That, I believe, is the real, true education. Beneath the façade of the person people think I am lies my true self.

The essence of which they would never realize, even in their most enlightened times of awareness and consciousness.

If only they knew the effluvium and scum I have had to swim through, maybe they would appreciate the fact that whatever falls into a salt mine would taste like salt, while essentially, it is not salt. When, occasionally, traces of scum and effluvium flush out of me, it is only a manifestation of the life I have been through.

A person is a combination of many things: his parental upbringing, the result of some predispositions inherited genetically from his ancestors, and the interaction of the society in which he thrives in. To put it briefly, a person is the result of a biological and cultural heritage.

I believe nature and nurture have made me what I am, a pessimistic member of the human race, a product of a weird and unstable family, an impulsive person conditioned to do things without seriously considering the implications. My upbringing never created the conditions where I was given the opportunity to discriminate for myself between good and bad, right or wrong, kindness or wickedness, love or hatred. I either had to take instructions or learn by instinct. My senses of values were distorted because I had no model to copy from. Like a chick without the mother hen to guide and protect, I had to learn the hard way. I did not know how to pick up the pieces of my disorganized life and restore some meaning to a seemingly meaningless life; I lack the confidence and fortitude to finish whatever I start. My early childhood insecurity keeps haunting me. My defenses cannot cope. I am like an open book for people to read, always at the mercy of people who take advantage of me.

Looking through the windows of my past life, my childhood memories come back to me with the biting pain of deep wounds, wounds that will never heal. Wounds that I believe will remain, afflicting my soul, even when my mortal body passes away. Rottenness has been the epitome and legacy of those tender years. Wasted years when my skinny physique made me look like a victim of malnutrition and tuberculosis. My hands clenched into fists by a feeling of insecurity normally sought succor below my chin. My head shook from side to side like a leaf. The whole saga of pain and neglect I had to go through were told in my terrified eyes-a description an aunt told me as I grew up.

As a child I was caught up in a nasty snowball rolling down the declivity of life's mountainous descent. A snowball created by the unholy alliance of a degenerate father with an unloving mother who hated me because of the color of my skin. Though both my parents were Israelis, I was a bit dark-complexioned for an Israeli. A fact I believe must be a biological inheritance from one of my ancestors.

But why should the pigments that determine the color of a child's skin deprive that child of her mother's milk, love, kindness, and attention?

III

I was born in Jerusalem in 1945. If my memory serves me right, the street I used to live on was called Mish Cannot, but what I do remember clearly about the street was that it contained a lot of little stones.

The entrance door of my grandfather's house was made from a narrow, heavy iron by which there was a balustrade measuring about two feet deep and three feet wide. The yellowish stones that the balustrade was made of looked like marble. The balustrade went beyond the iron door and terminated at the top of the staircase. The staircase and the area around it were always very eerie and dark. The stairs led into a square hall made of cold, hard cement. There was a window, six foot long and one foot wide, at the edge of the wall close to the ceiling where I could not see anything outside. It was not conspicuous.

As one entered the hall, on the right-hand corner was a door that led into my bedroom, where I spent most of my time. Inside the room was a communicating door that led to my grandfather's bedroom.

The house was bereft of any extravagance in furnishing. In fact, the only items of furniture I can remember were a bed and a small, old cabinet beside it in my room. My grandfather's room was the same, except he also had a sewing machine covered with a cloth, which served as a table for an old, brown radio.

I can't remember seeing any ornaments in the house, but there was something of interest in my bedroom that always fascinated me. It was a large carpet measuring about four feet wide and six feet long hanging on the wall behind my bed. The carpet had a pink and light blue background, and it displayed the impressive picture of a group of young ladies

7

dipping their feet into a little lake. Floating on the lake were a few white and pink swans.

Beyond the lake was another group of ladies, leaning on trees. Some of the ladies had children with them. The most outstanding feature of the picture on the carpeted wall, for me, was the long hair of the ladies portrayed in it. Some of them were blonde, others were brunette; the carpet was the most treasured thing that I had in those tender years. I used to stare at and study it for hours every day; I did not have any toys or anything to play with.

CHAPTER TWO

I

One afternoon, I was away from my bedroom which was something that did not happen often. I had wandered into the hall where I sat on the corner like a punished little girl playing on the floor.

My father, who had been out working, being a bus driver by profession and owning shares with that company, came back home. As he walked into the hall, he saw me and came toward me. He carried me in his arms and took me back to my bedroom where he dumped me on the bed.

I watched him remove his clothes, and then he left the room for a few minutes. When he returned, he brought back with him a bottle of oil which he applied on his private parts. He achieved an erection as he applied the oil to his penis.

This time, unlike the first occasion when he raped me, I was aware of what his intentions were, but there was nothing I could do about it. I took to crying because it was a very painful experience for me; but to no avail. He reached for me, turned me over on my tummy, and laid his bulk on me forcing his oiled penis between my buttocks and into my rectum. I screamed and shouted. He pressed my face hard on the dirty pillow, suppressing any noise I was making.

As on the previous occasion when he raped me, I bled from my buttocks and soiled the bed with excrement.

After a little while, still tormented by the pain that had been inflicted on me, I returned to the hall where I sat down on the corner crying and sobbing aloud.

After a while something unusual happened.

My father walked into the hall, put his hand into his pocket, and brought out something which he shoved into my mouth as if to say, "Get this into your dirty mouth and stop crying." At that time, I didn't realize what he had given me, except that it tasted nice. Later on, when I became older and looked back on that incident, I realized he had given me candy. It was an unusual experience because he had never given me anything before.

I saw very little of my grandfather in whose house my father and I lived. He was a man with a slight build, about five feet and three inches tall, slim, big brown eyes, and looked like a typical Yemenite, for he was; a humble-looking face with a thin, grey, straggly, long beard that thinned out down his jaw. He was caretaker of a school and an orthodox Jew who attended the synagogue regularly. He used to wake up as early as three or four o' clock in the morning to pray in a low whisper, walking slowly in and out of my bedroom. He normally had some strange cubes on his head which he rolled about with the aid of a phylactery.

One vivid memory I have of him is a song he used to sing quite often. The words ran thus: Ya lell, ya lell, ya, le le lee.

It was said my grandfather was a very strange person, whom, it was believed, drove his wife crazy to a point where she had to be put away in sanatorium.

There were times she disappeared from home for days only to be found in strange houses doing domestic work for no money.

I never met her when I was a child.

It remains a mystery to me why my grandfather never came near me or touched me. He carried on whatever he did without paying any attention to me. If he knew or suspected what transpired between my father and me when he was not at home, he did nothing about it.

Maybe he deliberately shied away from the sad truth that his son was a sick man. Or maybe he was oblivious of what was happening. I am sure he must have had some idea what sort of a person his son was.

In spite of the fact that he was remote from me, neither cuddling me or playing with me the way grandparents are inclined to do with their grandchildren, my memories of him are that of a very quiet and kind person.

It could be a good thing I did not get to know him and understand him better as a person. If I had, perhaps the fondness which I have for him as the only member of the family who didn't harm me would not exist.

I must have been about four or four-and-a-half years old. I remember my father had a small, black car. One afternoon, he drove me in the car to several places, presumably to get me into some kind of child care. He couldn't get me into the official government nursery because I was too young.

I also recall on that day that he had a very heated discussion with a group of women who did not appear to be convinced by what he told them about getting me a place in a nursery or something.

The picture of that day comes very clearly into my mind. It was a gloomy day, and the sun was not visible in the sky. The air was humid, making breathing very uncomfortable.

II

My little sister Debra is two years younger than I am. As children, she was normal whilst I was very skinny. Apart from the fact that we shared the same parents, we had very little in common with each other. I was dirty whilst she was clean. She had black curly hair, thinner lips than mine, big brown eyes, and a lighter skin complexion; a fact that probably made my mother more inclined to like her than myself. In contrast, I had straight black hair that looked Asiatic.

She was luckier than I was in many ways. When our parents were divorced, my mother took her along with her to Tel-Aviv, whilst I remained in my grandfather's home with my father.

Being a bus driver by profession, my father worked different shifts, both day and night. He had his own room where its entrance was from the outside next to the gate door.

He had the key to come upstairs when ever he felt like it. There were times he used to come home late at night, and he would wait downstairs for my grandfather to go to the synagogue. As soon as he heard him leave, he would open the metal door down stairs, and like a thief, would run up in a hurry into my room, he would wake me up and rape me from behind, suppressing my screams with his hand pressed over my mouth.

It is not quite clear to me if my father was supposed to share my bedroom with me, or whether he was supposed to sleep downstairs. But I know he always raped me whenever my grandfather was not at home. I was too frightened and terrified of my father to say or do anything about the pain he constantly inflicted on me.

At that stage of my life, I still could not comprehend whether or not the sodomy and incestuous affair he had with me was a normality that happened to every little child in other families.

After a while, I became so used to these sexual attacks that my sexual feelings were already aroused by the time I was six. Later on, whenever he came into my room to indulge himself, I used to ask him in tears to do it from the front. He always ignored me on these occasions. He was probably too scared of the consequences that might have followed such an undertaking if it be known that I had lost my virginity at so tender an age; or he simply enjoyed sodomy. I remember I used to take pieces of cloth, roll them together, and make it look like a penis, and tried to stimulate myself with it. I used to put the pieces of cloth by the bedside cabinet.

The only time when I think my sister, Debra, came closest to sampling the kind of treatment meted out me by our father was one occasion when she stayed with us for a few hours or a day.

She had been brought to stay there because our mother was attending to some pressing matters. I was sleeping on the bed with Debra, and my father was behind me. He inserted his penis into my backside whilst at the same time his hands fondled Debra's body. She must have been only about two years old then. I remember I started to cry in pain, and then we were both crying. My father did not attempt to rape her, probably because of the certainty that it would be detected by my mother.

Another of the few occasions I remember being in very close contact with Debra was in Tel Aviv. I do not remember the circumstances that took me there, but I recall my aunt Margol bathed the two of us and was scrubbing hard on our skins as she dried us with a towel. I was tickling my sister all over her body, and she was laughing uncontrollably.

One other occasion I do remember clearly was one afternoon left alone in the quiet, sordid existence of mine, lost in my imaginings. I realized there was a burst of activity downstairs.

Amidst frantic knocking and banging on the door, I heard a voice. I decided to find out who it was. I found my way slowly down the cold, thick, slippery, stone stairs and stood in front of a very small area by the narrow gate. The voice was saying that she was my mother and that my little sister, Debra, was with her. She asked me to look through the keyhole. It took me quiet a long time to understand what I was to do, at the end, I obeyed, and as I did that, she forced a few sweets to me through the keyhole before they departed. I cannot remember displaying any emotions of elation, or otherwise, as I sacked the candies.

Later that day, when my father was busy pacing down the hall and walking in and out of the shack-looking kitchen, I followed him around, asking him, "Where is mummy?" I was

15

mumbling, trying to tell him that she had been around. He replied casually that I had no mummy, she was dead.

On several occasions, he had tried to convince me I had no mother. I remember after the incident when my mother passed some candies to me through the narrow keyhole, she brought my little sister, Debra, to see me again. On that occasion, my mother searched for my grandfather, and when she found him, she tried hard to convince him to go against my father's wishes, asking him to let me go out so she could see me. She complained to him about my condition and how bad I looked. Debra was dressed very gorgeously and looked very happy. She spread out her dress nodding her body from left to right, showing off and repeating the word "America'" several times in a childish and innocuous manner, trying to convey to me the fact that the clothes she was wearing had been bought for her by my mother. My mother occasionally traveled to America. Whenever she did, she never bought anything for me.

CHAPTER THREE

I

I was a very lonely person when I was in the nursery. I did not mix freely and socialize with the other kids as they had fun playing on the swings, doing some paintwork on canvasses provided, or just running in circles. Instead, I was content with sitting on a stool close to a piano where I kept on pressing the keys and listening to the notes, wondering where the sound was going to, and why it disappeared. I would do that for hours until my teacher would lift me off the stool and ask me to go and play with the other kids. Because I was so happy and absorbed with the piano, I struggled vigorously, kicking my legs in the air and wriggling my shoulders. Playing with the other kids was not a substitute for the peace of mind I achieved from the piano.

That experience, when I sat down and pressed the keys of the piano, was very significant for me. It was my first introduction to music, although it was a very superficial one.

II

I was playing one afternoon in the streets outside when I saw my father coming out of the house with a blonde woman. She was quite attractive. I guess in her mid-twenties with a hairstyle that suited her. Over the forehead were three or four finger waves that went backwards, and at the back, her hair was pinned down. I nodded a greeting to her. She returned the gesture as she passed by. Later on, when I got to know her better, she told me that on that particular occasion she had asked my father who I was, and his reply was that I was a no-one.

She later moved into the house and became my stepmother when my father married her.

In many ways her marriage to my father marked a turning point in my life; my father isolated himself with her in the room downstairs. He found pleasure with his new woman and stop raping me. The marriage also opened to me a new vista of experience that was a hitherto unknown to me. I began to do things under supervision.

She used to put a wooden box in front of the sink so that I could reach and wash the dirty dishes. I was still a very little girl then, perhaps five years old; still, it did not stop her using me like a slave child.

I was very dirty from want of being washed, coupled with the fact that my timidity made me an object of ridicule for the kids living around. They used to pour sand all over me; it was not surprising I had lice on my head.

My stepmother asked me to sit down in front of her while she removed the lice individually. I was so touched and emotionally moved by that experience that I called her mother. To a child like me, deprived of love and affection, I regarded her as my mother because of her act of kindness in removing the lice from my head. She reflected on what I had called her for a while and replied that she was not really my mother. She said it would be sufficient if I just called her auntie. At that stage of my life, I had wanted her to be my mother. When she continued to remove the lice, my father noticed she spent a few hours doing it; he said to shave my entire head. My stepmother replied by saying maybe it would be a better idea if she tried to kill the lice by applying petrol to my hair. She tried the petrol treatment, but it didn't seem to eradicate the lice, so after two days, my hair was shaved and covered with a scarf. I was about six years old then and had to go to school like that. It was my first year at school. The kids used to make fun of my head, each lifting the scarf in turn, and saying funny things about my shaven head. I was subject to this for several months because it took some time for my hair to grow to a reasonable length. I had to cope with the unsavory experience of my head being shaved again, because at school and whenever I played outside the house, I got very dirty playing with sand and having it poured on me by dirty children who played around.

III

During my first year at school, I made little or no progress. I used to sit in the class and daydream. I would stare at the teacher, not to understand what was being said, but to marvel at the way the chalk ran on the blackboard. I was impervious to the learning process. Being so wrapped up in my thoughts, I felt numb that the teacher could not help discussing my lack of progress with my father. They considered the possibility of putting me into a school for mentally retarded children. It would appear that my stepmother had intervened and put a stop to it. She did not want to lose the slave child. I don't think my father was compassionate enough to have made such a decision.

It would have been a paradise for me to have strangers looking into my problems trying to help me.

I was so backward at that time, that at night, I used to wet my bed, and my father used to hit me quite hard on the buttocks with his hands, leaving deep, red marks, telling me to do it in the right place instead of in my bed.

CHAPTER FOUR

I

When I was about seven years old, we moved out of the house, leaving my grandfather's house in Jerusalem to occupy a new one my father had bought in the Shikun Havatikim. The Shikun Havatikim was composed of mainly residential quarters. It was a new development section on the outskirts of Jerusalem on top of the mountains and close to mount Herzzel. The quarters were still undergoing construction when we moved in.

The houses in the quarters were painted white; our house was a two family house. The builders left a lot of heaps of gravel, sand, stones, and garbage that mounted all the way up to the front door where we had to force our way into the house. We had to clear it to make a garden.

My stepmother told me that on the onset my father did not want me to move with them; he told her that he preferred it if I stayed with my grandfather. I do not know if my stepmother had some sympathy for me and thought otherwise. I think maybe at the back of her mind, lay the thought that I was, and would remain, handy with the domestic work like cleaning, washing, and sweeping that I was always engaged in.

Work played a vital part in my life at that time. In a world devoid of parental love and the trappings of the average family, work was psychologically rewarding for me. I always had something to do. It made me think less about the absence of things like toys and beautiful clothes in my life. My clothes were always bought second-hand, and more often than not, they were too big for me. I had to put on a belt most of the time so that the dresses would look reasonable on me. I was told that I would "grow into them." My shoes also were not the right size; they were much too big and flopped on and off when I walked. My father always maintained that it would save him from buying a new pair each year.

I used to be woken up as early as three or four o'clock in the morning to help decongest the backyard. I had to fill a rubber bucket with the rubbish and walk about half a mile to dump it.

In addition to this, I did the normal domestic work in the house. The routine overtaxed my abilities when I later registered with a school about two months after we moved to the Shikun.

Engaged in the strenuous activity I did everyday, I used to be drained of all energy. I often went to school very late and slept through most of the periods at school.

To add to my predicament, I had to trek about two to three miles to and from school.

The other kids who lived in the vicinity would taunt and mock me, at times calling me a black slave because they saw how hard I worked. I complained about them to my stepmother, and I also mentioned the fact that I was always late for school. She promised to talk to the parents of the kids concerned, but she didn't seem to bother about my being late for school. My teacher, who lived only a few houses away, complained about my habitual lateness and sleeping in class, but somehow the blame was put on me. I was portrayed as a lazy child who was prone to sleeping and clumsiness.

Thereafter, my stepmother used to put me to bed much earlier, but the domestic routine I did in the mornings remained unchanged. When I returned from school, I picked up where I left off in the morning. I washed dishes, scrubbed the floors, and at times washed some of her clothes, including her monthly period underwear.

I became even skinnier than I was before.

My father, who was always very mean with food even though he was not a poor man, always ensured that I had very little to eat; even the olives I ate had to be counted.

I remember one day my stepmother prepared some meatballs and put them in the fridge. I was very hungry and too frightened to ask for permission to help myself with some of it, so I decided to steal a little from each one, innocently thinking she would not notice. She was furious with me when she realized what I had done. I was scolded very severely on that occasion.

On another occasion, she saw me counting some silver coins. She asked me where I had gotten them. I replied that my auntie called Rachel, whom I used to spend certain weekends with, had given them to me. She slapped me and interrogated me continuously about how much Rachel gave to me and how long ago it was.

That night, after I had already gone to bed, I was woken up when my father came back home from work. For my stepmother, it was not enough that she had already slapped me, she had to go and tell my father what had happened. Without giving me a chance to say anything, my father started flogging me with a belt.

Like always when I was punished, I was locked in the bathroom and forced to sleep in the cold bathtub.

My first real attempt at forging a friendship with a girl about my age in my first year at school foundered very prematurely. She was different from most of the other kids whose company I seldom kept because I was too shy and my communication skills were less than zero. She appeared to like me as much as I liked her.

In the course of what I thought was our friendship, I confided in her by asking her if her father used to go to her bed and put his penis in her rectum. She just stared at me puzzled, and I continued to describe in detail what my father did to me. Deep inside me there raged a conflict as to whether or not what had happen to me was normal. I wanted to know how she would feel about it. In next to no time, she spread the news around the school to the other kids who then mocked, scorned, and made me an object of severe ridicule. Even at that age, the betrayal of a friend was disappointing. I was not going to allow the betrayal to go unpunished.

My juvenile mind sought a way of retribution. My chance came when she was alone in the playground one break time. I went over to her without warning her of my intentions, pushed her on the ground, sat on her, and started beating and banging her head on the hard surface in the process.

She yelled in pain but I was relentless. I wanted to even the score; she had caused me undue embarrassment by disclosing to everyone my father's sexual experiences with me. As I punished her, the other kids soon became aware of what was happening and attracted the attention of the teacher by their screams and stampeding.

Though I felt relieved over what I had done to the girl, the embarrassment and ordeal she made me go through drove home to me the full impact of how unacceptable it was for my father to have done what he did to me. Otherwise, why had I been humiliated by it? I knew it was wrong of him to do that, but my incapacity as a child didn't allow me to appreciate that it takes all types to make up the world. The good, the bad, and the very bad have to coexist.

That incident made me further isolated in the school. My teacher thought my presence in the school was undesirable. She probably thought I was an empty-headed, incorrigible, and problematic child whose influence would be bad on the other kids. Little did she realize I was a victim of circumstance, a bad specimen of what nature and nurture can do to a little girl.

Due to the fighting incident, I was suspended which later terminated my stay there.

One morning, I woke up feeling very uneasy in the insides of my mouth. I felt a burning sensation inside. It happened again the next day, so I told my stepmother about it. She said she had put hot pepper all over my thumb when I had gone to bed to stop me from sucking my thumb, which I often did in the night. This pepper treatment continued for a while until I stopped sucking my thumb.

My life was drab most of the time. Nothing exciting really happened within the family. We went through life as though it was an obstacle course. The few rays of sunshine that shone on my life came from the weekend visits I paid to Aunt Rachel. She lived in an historical, comfortable, old fashion house. I usually partook with her family in the traditional Friday dinner cooked in the Yemenite Spanish way.

Although their attitude toward me was not very warm, I cherished the food they treated me to, especially the carp fish, chicken and rice, and tomato and garlic.

There were times when I was the topic of after dinner conversation for my paternal relatives who were always around at Aunt Rachel's. They usually talked derisively about my father, making fun of him, mimicking how timid and unintelligent they thought he was.

In later life, I questioned why I was allowed to stay with my father whilst my relatives knew what sort of cruel and mean man my father was; my grandmother had replied by saying that in my early childhood, Aunt Rachel had taken me away from my mother and returned me to my father in Jerusalem.

This feature, in keeping me within the paternal side of the family, had been done to maintain the prestige of my father's family. My mother's answer was another way of my grandmother saying if I hadn't been taken away by my paternal side of the family, they would have taken care of me somehow.

II

My two best friends, Eilana and Zehava, were sisters. They were aged ten and eleven respectively. We were all classmates. Zehava should have been studying in a class one year lower, but she was demoted because she was a dullard. Her sister, Eilana, was not bright either, but she had a more pleasant personality than her sister. They lived only down the street from me. On certain Saturdays the three of us used to play together and walk down the mountain near Encarem to pick poppies, cyclamen, and nice mountain flowers. We also used to go to Mount Herzzel which is known as the famous burial place of the soldiers who fought for the independence of Israel. On the way to Mount Herzzel there were a few fig trees where we often climbed to eat figs. We made sure that they did not have maggots by splitting each fig in half.

The parents of Eilana and Zehava were very kind to me. I used to confide in them about how I was treated at home. They were very sympathetic. They told me there were times they greeted my father on the street, but he had often ignored them. They thought he was a very strange man. I suppose at that time they must have thought he was rude because he didn't reply.

In later life, I learned that he was very hard of hearing and couldn't have heard any greeting from anyone.

I sometimes used to eat with the two sisters whenever I paid them a visit. We had a mutual friend who lived about a mile away. On Friday evening, we used to go get her and practice dance steps in the streets. We also used to sing Israeli folk songs and play games like hopscotch and skipping. On Friday afternoons at school, during the last hour before we departed, we used to take out chairs and arrange them in a circle. Then we would sing and clap. They used to ask me to sing solo. At times, I would do it willingly, at other times, I would hesitate. Whenever I did hesitate, the children would say I did it deliberately so that they would have to beg me to sing. They liked my voice and the way I sang. We had a favorite Yemenite singer called Shoshana Damari whose songs we always liked to sing.

The kids sometimes put on one of her records and I would sing along with it; then they played games by lowering down the volume slowly and at times then high again. The synchronization of my voice with that of the singer was quite remarkable. These social activities must have helped me considerably. I remember my teacher who took me aside in Hebrew and History to praise my progress. I was proud to find some of my short stories hanging on the walls of the classroom. The teacher once remarked that she thought I had a lot of imagination.

When my stepsister, Yemet, was born, the household was in a state of frenzy. I became even more domesticated than I was before.

One day my stepmother told me that my mother wanted to see me. I was quite baffled and confused because my father had repeatedly told me she was dead. I felt very strange and uneasy. I had gotten used to her not being around.

The fact that she wanted to see me sounded like an impossible dream, as unintelligible as the moon coming down to me. I later realized she was with a middle-aged couple who lived about a mile away. They were very simple and friendly.

I didn't quite recognize my mother when I saw her. She was very attractive. About five-feet three inches tall, little fairer than me in complexion, with curly black hair. Her nose was typically Jewish, exceptionally long. "Ruthi, come here," she said to me as I stared at her blankly. She stared at me for a long time, seemingly bewildered as if meeting me for the first time. After an uneasy silence, she remarked that I looked very emaciated and ill. She reached for her bag and passed me a bar of chocolate.

In a way, her visit was a unique experience for me. She talked at length about how bad I looked and promised I was going to spend my next summer holidays with her in Tel Aviv.

I had very strange experience with the son of a neighbor who was very friendly with my stepmother. Because my stepmother and his mother paid each other visits, I became friendly with him. He was one of the very backward boys in my class. One day, when my stepmother had gone out, there was nothing unusual when he knocked on the door and I let him in.

Things seemed to happen very fast. He removed his shorts and asked me to hold his penis. I was about to do it when he panicked, struggled into his shorts, and left the room in a hurry.

After that incident, I saw very little of him. Whenever our eyes met either in class or elsewhere, he always avoided my gaze.

III

The next summer holidays, I traveled to see my mum. Because my father was a bus driver, I had a pass to travel free on certain routes. She lives in the middle of the Yemenite quarters in Tel Aviv, which was really a slum area that was primitively built.

When I arrived, I met my maternal cousins who gave me a rousing reception. At first, they did not know who I was, but then, when they found out that I was Ruthi, Yona's daughter, they all went hysterical. They stampeded with excitement. I joined them in the euphoria that ensued.

It was a very enjoyable holiday, but it appeared to go too quickly. The only black spot in it was what happened when I told my mother I wanted to stay with her. I didn't want to go back to my father. She insisted I must go back. I remember when I protested, she chased me in the streets with a stick, swearing at me, and losing her sandals in the process.

There was a youth movement in the vicinity which attracted a lot of youngsters. The meetings of this movement were held on Friday evenings. They served as a forum that promoted the interests of the kids; a place where the young could participate in several activities and interact with other children. I wanted to join this movement as a fully-fledged member, so every Friday after evening meals, I would ask my stepmother if I could attend. She used to consult my father who would allow me to go after expressing some reluctance. But as time went on, he refused permission for me to go, because, according to him, there were boys in it. He feared I would be corrupted. He often said when the time came he would find the right man for me to marry.

CHAPTER FIVE

I

My breasts started to develop at the age of eleven. I was very conscious and shy about it. I would normally tie a piece of a long narrow cloth around my body to flatten the mounds of my breasts.

Every now and then, on my way back from school, the boys would taunt me and try to pull it away. The boys didn't seem to like me. At that time, I thought it could have something to do with my looks. I often thought a fringe hairstyle suited me very well, but my stepmother thought otherwise. She preferred my hair to be parted on the sides and pushed down.

The development of my breasts remained a source of grave concern to me. I began to figure out, subconsciously, that my father may begin to get ideas about me again. To avoid such occurrences, I started dropping some subtle hints about the virtues of living in a kibbutz. I thought it would be the ideal place for me.

According to the neighbors, one needs no particular qualifications to go, except that one had to be of the right age. One would combine living there with working and learning as most members of the youth movements around did. Moreover, the social life there was supposed to be very healthy. The thought of going there fascinated me.

My father was strongly against what the entire kibbutz stood for. By his way of thinking, he reckoned it would give him a very bad reputation if he allowed me to go into a kibbutz. He would be seen in the eyes of society as a man who was shirking his responsibilities as a father. I reminded him of people like Moshe Dayan and Ben Gurion who were great men, yet as they were products of the kibbutz system. He dismissed what I said with contempt.

After a lot of persistent persuasion, he finally gave in. I went to a special office where the formalities of registering, choosing a special kibbutz, and arranging the date of departure were concluded.

On the appointed day of departure to the kibbutz, I had to be in the bus station to start the first leg of the journey from Jerusalem to Tel Aviv. I met some other kids of my own age group bound for the same kibbutz at the main bus station. There were two guides, both named Tsvika, distinguished by the prefix fat and slim. They were to ensure we arrived safely. When we got to Tel Aviv, we boarded another bus to Afulah.

Ma'Oz Hayyim, our kibbutz, was situated in Emek Bet Shean, reputedly, one of the hottest areas in Israel. I enjoyed the interaction with the other children. It was a welcome change from the humdrum kind of existence I had come to know. The kibbutz was well-organized, and the discipline there was quite remarkable. In the mornings, I used to work picking grapes. There was a tractor in the kibbutz that towed a large, rectangular platform on wheels. We worked five days a week. We would meet on a designated place, jump for the platform, and sit as it drove through the fields. I recall during one of those times we spent working on the fields, I saw a two-foot-long snake about one to two inches wide. I was frightened by it. We worked from 4:00 a.m. to 7:00 a.m. in the morning, after which, the tractor took us to the restaurant where all the members of the kibbutz assembled to eat. The food was wheeled around in trolleys; everyone took whatever appealed to their taste. The diet was balanced. Amongst many other things, we had a creamy -like Shamenet yogurt, salads, fruits, and vegetables. There was also a laundry where we washed our clothes. I sometimes was allocated to work there. I shared a room with three other girls. Most of the things there, like clothing and shoes, were free.

There was a marked improvement in my work at school. My outlook on life through my foggy, dreamy mind seemed a little bit brighter. In that period of my life, I did not realize it, and did not appreciate. And instead of taking advantage of my new life for improving my education, my mental health, and peace of mind, I was just existing and did not know the meaning of life and what is all about. The time used to pass quickly which was an indication that I was enjoying myself, trying helplessly to adjust to a normal life.

After spending about a year in the kibbutz, I went to spend my holidays with my mother in Tel Aviv. While on holiday, I was told that one of my male cousins called Schlomi, who was about two years senior to me, was in another kibbutz. He was in Lohame Haghettaot which means, "The men who fought in the ghettoes," and the place was a tribute to the Jewish survivors of Nazi oppression. I was persuaded to move to my cousin's kibbutz. When I went back to Ma'Oz Hayyim, I asked for a transfer, but my instructor tried to dissuade me. He appeared to be the only person to like me at that time of my life, and I was very flattered by it. Still, I did not listen to his good advice, I paved my life toward a big disaster, which was one of the biggest mistakes of my life. Still, I made up my mind to leave. One day, I do not know why, I decided I must go, so I moved out unceremoniously.

The kids in my new kibbutz were older than me by two or three years. I made new friends, and with the passage of time, I came to like a boy named Yehiell who was one of the very clever ones in my class. I always talked about him and tried to get his attention, but my feelings were not reciprocated. He was interested in other girls and only gave me a fleeting attention.

After a while, my feelings of liking for him gradually died. For weeks, he started to yearn for my friendship, but, by then, my liking for him had turned to cold indifference.

Every Friday, our group used to have folk dancing in the kibbutz.

One Friday evening, there was a dance in the kibbutz in which I completely ignored him, preferring the company of a Spanish-looking boy who was a sharp contrast to the rest of us. His name was Butcha-cha, brash and sophisticated-looking, both in his manner and clothing. He made the rest of us look ordinary. I was with him throughout the dance. During the dance, some of kids kept coming into the dancing room, calling me to come out and talk to Yehiell. First, they told me that he was asking me to dance with him, and I ignored him. Then, they continued to come in and out asking me repeatedly to go out because he wanted to talk to me. I just do not know why I behaved the way I did.

Later that night, when I had returned to bed with three other girls with whom I shared a room, we were woken up by the light that was switched on and the children who burst into my room. One of the boys was a friend of Yehiell, the boy I no longer cared for. According to him, Yehiell had gone to the cattle shed after the dance. Wondering what he was up to, he had followed him there. It transpired that Yehiell had tried to kill himself with a chisel he had picked up in the cattle shed. He persuaded Yehiell not to commit suicide and gave him some money to go home. Asked why he had wanted to kill himself, he replied by saying, it was because his love for me was not reciprocated.

The boy who woke us up later broke the news to the other kids who made quite a big thing about it. That night, there was a rumpus as the kids blamed me and heaped abuses on me for letting Yehiell attempt to commit suicide.

I could hardly sleep that night. I felt very depressed, not by my feelings of guilt, but by the verbal chastisement I received from everyone.

The next morning, I work up a miserable wreck. When I went to work, I did things mechanically without any real feelings. I couldn't eat breakfast and couldn't concentrate on what I was doing. Downtrodden, I decided to walk aimlessly into the fields. I walked sheepishly, wondering why such terrible things happened to me. I was very dizzy and dejected.

I wandered into a place where the tractors got filled with petrol. The place was very quiet, so I decided to go to the tank where petrol was stored. I opened the tap and started to drink petrol. I took several pints of it, until I became helpless and let myself foul on the ground. I can't remember how long I remained on the ground, but I noticed a man walking toward me. He was a middle-aged, average built man with ginger-colored hair. He asked me what I was doing on the ground. I replied by saying, "I have been drinking petrol." At first, he did not believe my story. I kept pointing into my mouth and keep begging him to smell my mouth and chase where the petrol dripped on me, but once he had established the truth for himself by smelling my mouth and my clothes, he called for help. Though there was a clinic in Lohame Hagetaot, I was rushed to the hospital in Afulah, where a long tube was inserted in my mouth and down my throat. A sickening feeling made me vomit most of the petrol I had drunk into a metal bowl held out by one of the nurses.

When I returned to the kibbutz, word about my attempted suicide had already gone around. The kids taunted me, telling me that I was going to be taken into a sanatorium because I was mentally unstable.

I was later taken to Afulah where I had an appointment with a female psychiatrist. She asked me why I had wanted to kill myself, and what my family relationship was like. I did not mention anything about my family to her; the children's threats about me going to a mental hospital made me frightened and worried what the consequences would be. My only reply to her questions was that I did what I did because of a love affair. She came to the conclusion that I needed to be loved at home, so, by her recommendation, I was to be sent home.

A telegram was sent to my home requesting my father should come and take me back. I protested to my instructor why I didn't want to go home. It was because I hated my father.

When my father arrived to take me away, the instructor told me that he could not understand why I didn't like him. I took to my heels, running into the fields. I was pursued by a middle-aged member of the kibbutz. When I was caught, the instructor questioned me with a stern voice as to why I didn't want to go home. I was tongue-tied because I was too frightened of my father to utter any syllable.

All the way back home on the bus toward Jerusalem, I quietly cried my eyes out. I remembered my father, in a strange and stupefied way, asked me why I was crying. I was too terrified and so frightened of him; to me he was like a big, giant beast. I could not confront him. I was even afraid to stare at him when he talked to me that day on the bus; I only gave him a quick glance and did not say anything to him. I just kept crying as though I would have to hold the whole world on my shoulders when I was only fourteen years old.

After about two days in Jerusalem, I told him I wanted to go to college. Having stayed in a kibbutz these few years, I had come to cherish going to school and the education that goes along with it. I was starving to learn.. My father replied by saying if I gave in to his sexual demands, he may consider buying me the books. My eyes were on a good college in En Carem, which it was located from our home, halfway to the center of Jerusalem. I pleaded with him so many times but to no avail.

Since I couldn't go to a college, I registered to attend evening classes in a night school in the centre of Jerusalem. My stay in the night school proved to be very short in light of what happened to me when I came back to my father.

It started one morning when I woke up with a start. I was being kissed passionately on the lips. I discovered it was my father. I threatened I was going to scream if he didn't go away. He left reluctantly. Early the next morning, he came back again. This time it was more difficult to get rid of him. After breakfast, I tried to tell my stepmother about what was happening, but I could not summon enough courage to do so. She pressed that I tell her, but I could not. I decided to run off. I took a bus to Tel Aviv to my grandmother.

I also complained to my mother, who lived just a stone's throw away from my grandmother. I also told them what my father used to do to me when I was a little child.

My mother then added that she recalled, when I was about two and a half years old, she had walked into the house unexpectedly after chatting with a neighbor and had found my father lying on the bed, naked, with his hands stretched high, carrying me, his penis erect in front of him. She asked him, "Shalom, what are you doing?" He threw me on the bed saying, "Ho, nothing, nothing." That revelation by my mother actually hit me like a heavy tree. It told me, more than anything else could, that all along my mother knew what kind of person my father was, and had wittingly allowed me to stay with him. She didn't care about my welfare. If she did, she would have ensured I was not left with a man who was capable of incestuous relations with his daughter. Looking back, I think it was a stupid thing for her to tell me. She betrayed my trust, and as she was such a selfish woman, later on I found out that her mother loved and spoiled her more than all her other children. Therefore, she did get the love, care, and affection, but she was not capable of giving me even a very small piece of that.

My grandmother started cursing in Arabic, in a primitive way, and told me to go back to Jerusalem and complain to my stepmother about what I had told them. She thought it was their problem in Jerusalem. In a way, my grandmother and mother were happy that something was going wrong on the other side of the family. They thrived on scandals, and it was a good thing that there was one in the offering.

I went back to Jerusalem, that night, but I did not go straight home. I went straight to night school, where in the middle of the class, I was called out. My stepmother wanted to know where I had been all day. I said nowhere and promised to come back home as soon as the evening classes were over.

My father happened to be on a nightshift that night. That afforded me the opportunity to tell my stepmother everything. She was crying and sobbing as she listened to my story. She said she had always suspected all was not right with him. There were times he used to lock himself up in the toilet for such a long time. On one occasion, she had peeped through the keyhole of the toilet and found him masturbating.

II

The deep concern and feeling of disappointment displayed by my stepmother over my father's unbecoming conduct was not so much over the emotional, mental, and physical strains I had been subjected to by my father's advances, but more over the fact that she had a daughter from him. She feared that if he could do that to me, her daughter was also exposed to that kind of peril. My stepmother advised me to lock my room whenever I went to bed. This was short-lived, because after only a few days, I wanted to lock the room, and to my amazement, the key went missing. I told my stepmother about it, she looked at me confused, and told me not to worry. Later on, she called me and pointed to my father's jacket. She put her hand inside his pocket, lifting the key, and saying, "Look, look where he put the key." Stupefied, I did not know what to say, so I asked her what should I do now. She was nervous about the whole scenario and replied that I continue to lock the door.

In a bid to get something done about this new state of affairs that had come to light, my stepmother decided to complain to her sister and her brother-in-law who lived in the town, about my father's conduct. I accompanied her there. My stepmother could not stop crying, my father's relations were in two minds whether or not to believe what I had said. In the end, her brother-in-law suggested that if we had anything to prove, we should go to the police. That was exactly what we did.

A police officer interrogated me about the allegations I made against my father. During the interrogation, I was giggling. I guess I was ashamed, shy, and did not know how I was supposed to conduct myself. I did not realize how important and serious it was for me to cooperate by being open and not so afraid, a fact, I believe, must have weakened the strength of my allegations. He could not comprehend my casual approach toward so serious an issue. My behavior was motivated by two main reasons. The first was that what my father did to me was my very first childish recollection, something I had had to live with as I grew up. It was not something sudden, like if a normal woman was attacked, raped, and was in a state of a shock. A woman like that would react in a completely different manner. To me, it was part of my life. Although I new it was wrong, I could not comprehend and understand. Therefore, I giggled to cover my shame as he interrogated me.

Secondly, although I knew the police were people in authority, I didn't appreciate at the time that they could actually do anything about my condition. So when they suggested that one of them hide somewhere in my house in an attempt to trap him red-handed while he tried to seduced me, I hesitated for a while, and in the end, I dismissed the idea because I was too frightened of my father. My stepmother also had her misgivings about such a plan. She pointed out that my father owned a gun, by virtue of the fact that he sometimes drove by bus along some dangerous routes, and he, therefore, had a license to carry and own a gun. If he was aware of the existence of a plot to trap him, he might use the gun.

Though the police said they had nothing concrete to work on, they found out something about my father's past life. They had a file on my father in the station. As a teenager, he worked in a movie theater, where, one day, he had raped a girl in the theater where he worked in the middle of Jerusalem, by switching off the lights after a film show.

In the end, the police suggested we return home. Later that night, my father came home, and a violent argument ensued between him and my stepmother. Apparently, the police had picked him up and taken him to the station for interrogation as he drove into Jerusalem. The next day, we all went to the police station, where my father repeatedly proclaimed his innocence. To add some credence to his case, he suggested to the police that, while I was in the kibbutz, I must have lost my virginity. He said this deliberately, knowing I was still a virgin, and he knew that this would free him because it would be hard to prove that he sodomized me when I was a little girl. Once it was proven that I was a virgin, his innocence would be apparent. And that was precisely what happened. He was able to manipulate the police, and me, to his own ends. I was taken to a hospital where the virginity test on me proved positive. My father was off the hook.

When we got home, there was a big row between my father and me. He tried to hit me whenever I maintained he had assaulted me sexually in the past and that he was still trying seducing me. He said if I continued to say these things, he would put me in a sanatorium. My stepmother's brother-in-law, who was participating in the ordeal, tried to intervene, but my father was too angry to take heed. In the end, my stepmother's brother-in-law advised me to leave the house and go to my mother's.

I was only fifteen years old then and in the mercy of who knows whom. I packed my few belongings and got ready to travel to Tel Aviv in search of a home, not knowing if my mother would accept me or not. When I boarded the bus that night, I had the feeling I was on a journey to the unknown. I was a helpless little girl; the word insecurity did not even exist in my vocabulary. As always, I was not down-to-earth with what was going on with me; ostracized from the kibbutz, having to go home to have care and love on the advice of a psychologist. On coming home, I am denied, ridiculed, abused, and instead of that very love I needed, I received a punishment of hate.

III

After my departure from Jerusalem due to the trouble that ensued between my father and me, my mother did not want me to stay with her. According to her, she didn't think her husband would like the idea.

My mother was married to Yemenite Jewish man who grow up in the United States. He was very selfish, mean, and stingy. He could not care or accept me, or my sister, Debra. He had two children from my mother, whom it would appear he did not particularly show much affection to, let alone some attention, but he obviously accepted them because they were his children.

He had no connection or communication with his other children from his previous marriage who were living in the United States. He treated my sister and I like scum.

I had begged endlessly and cried until I persuaded my mother that I had nowhere to go to if she refused for me to stay with her. I had promised to do all of her domestic work no matter what it was. That was the only way for me to persuade her to let me stay. It was an unpopular decision because her husband took a very dim view to it.

In spite of everything, I was relieved I was there. Anything was better than staying with my father. I found my mother a sharp contrast from my stepmother whom I had grown accustomed to living with. While my stepmother came from a stable and enlightened family who seem to view things liberally, my mother's family was backward, primitive, and most of the time out of touch with reality.

I spent most of my time with my grandmother who was very religious. She had a very large room downstairs in an isolated area, which she converted into a synagogue for the use of the Yemenite neighborhood community. She once told me that one of the conditions she laid down before she agreed to get married was that a synagogue would be in her matrimonial home.

She also leased part of the house to be a bakery where bread and hot rolls were always readily available. I remembered, in those days quite often, me, my sister, and cousins used to go downstairs to the bakery in the mornings to get some hot rolls.

From the instigation of my mother, who wanted me to go to work and earn money, I got a job in a delicatessen shop. The pay was next to nothing, so I had to look for another job. I got one in a factory in Jaafa, an industrial area. The owner of the factory was trying to seduce me, so my stay there was short-lived. Thereafter, I gave up the idea of working.

I used to socialize quite a lot, attending parties with my younger sister, Debra, who was then in the secondary school. She kept nagging me to take her along with me.

In spite of the fact that my grandmother, who disliked me partially because of my slightly darker skin, was accusing me quite often, telling me that I was a bad person, she blamed me for trying to corrupt Debra and ruin her. She repeatedly told me not to come to her house anymore, if I took Debra with me.

She used to shout all the time and curse a lot in Arabic. I got used to her screaming and cursing and just ignored her, like everybody else in the family. She loved my sister. My sister Debra was treated better than anyone else in the family, partly because she had a lighter skin color. The discrimination in my family played a big role.

I had about six maternal cousins in Tel Aviv, three boys and three girls. They used to visit my grandmother where I used to stay quite a lot. One day, one of the boys, who was about eighteen years old, tried to kiss me. In a fit of rage, I had bitten him severely on his cheek with my teeth. The bite made quite a deep impression on his face. I think he liked me quite a lot. It took several months before the scar on his face disappeared. My other cousins used to laugh at him, but neither he nor I revealed the fact that I had inflicted the bite on him. After that experience, he kept away from me.

One of my female cousins, who was a year younger than I was, was a showoff who thought she had in her make up the ingredients that would make her a singing star when she was of age. She had an exaggerated idea of her beauty.

One day, she told me she was going to see a music composer called Nardi.

Because this music composer had a bad reputation with girls, my cousin wanted me to go with her so as to deter him if he had any ideas about her. Without hesitation, I agreed to go with her. The music composer lived on the outskirts of Tel Aviv. He was a smallish-looking man of about five feet three inches, a Jew from Russia, but who had stayed in Israel for the best part of his life. He was nudging fifty-five. A very talented man whose songs were part of the Israeli folk music,

49

he had the deep, penetrating eyes of a deep-thinker. He had very thick hair, and it didn't seem to bother him that it was grey.

He sat at a piano, singing with a girl when we arrived at his place. The girl sang several songs with him while we just sat there on his sofa and admired his skill at the piano. After a while, he asked my cousin what songs she knew how to sing. When she had decided on the repertoire, she sang loudly and without any feelings or emotion. Nardi accompanied her with his artistic way of playing the piano. After she sang quite a few songs while I was listening, being quiet and shy, to my surprise, he asked me if could sing. Staring at him, stupefied, I told him that I was not sure, maybe I could sing a little. I mentioned to him some of the songs I knew. As I sang them, he played the piano in accompaniment.

Later, when I was alone with him in the kitchen making tea, he asked me if I could come and see him alone the next day. He reckoned I had a lot of talent, and that he would like to train me to sing properly, rather than my cousin or the other girl that was there who did not have any talent. He told me that my cousin only shouted. I was overwhelmed by what he said, I did not mention anything to my cousin, and kept secretive.

The next day, I went to his house. There, we did a few songs together; it was my very first discovery that I had a lot of talent as a singer. He told me he had a weakness for female, Yemenite singers. Within his view, they have the heart, soul, and emotions to provide great sounds. That accounted for his interest in my talent. He had helped, in the past, to build up a few famous Israeli Yemenite singers, and that was what he intended to do with me.

Nardi introduced me to classical music, which open my imaginations to sounds, notes, and also opened deepings into my heart and soul. He mentioned to me that I was the first Yemenite singer he knew that liked and appreciated classical music. He took me to see several concerts, and I was flabbergasted with joy and happiness.

I loved and enjoyed what he called hard work, which to me, was a child's game. One day, Nardi complimented me for learning twenty songs in one day. When he used to play the piano, coaching me, there were times he used to scream at me trying to correct some mistakes I was making. He wanted me to sing like his ex-wife when she was a big star in Israel. After only about two and a half months, I had done, to nearly perfection, ten children's songs, ten country songs, and ten military songs.

This, my early interest in music, which started in the nursery when, out of curiosity, I pressed the keys of the piano, was consummated by the nurturing Nardi gave me.

My first shot at public entertainment was a few months later when I starred with him at a university in Tel Aviv. I got a lot of praise and encouragement from a lot of people who appreciated my talent.

As the months progressed, my affection for my music composer, Nardi, grew from strength to strength. There were times I took him to my grandmother's place. He suffered from high blood pressure. I took care of him as much as I could, cleaning his house and doing odd jobs for him. My grandmother got suspicious of our relationship. She thought we were lovers, and because of the age difference, didn't like the idea. Despite the fact that I was very close to him, he never took advantage of me sexually. I was still a virgin.

My mother also frowned at, and did not approve of, what she thought was my strange liaison with a much older man. She wanted me to do some work and earn some money, not because she wanted to see me improve myself, but because she wanted the money for herself. She felt as a daughter, I owed her something.

It seems ironic, that, in spite of her lack of interest in my welfare as a child, she wanted and expected something from me. To sustain our relationship, the music composer paid me some money for helping with the music, and of course, it should have been the other way around. Whatever he paid, I handed over to my mother. I considered myself very fortunate because his other pupils paid him to coach them.

Our relationship continued to blossom. I used to accompany him to his sister's house where we were often treated to meals. His sister, like many others, was very skeptical about our relationship because of the age difference. I was only sixteen, and he was fifty-five or near there.

I told him everything about my early childhood, and he seemed sympathetic. I yearned for his affection. I would often stay in his house and sleep in his bed. Like an innocent little girl, I wanted to be cuddled, patted on the head, and kissed on my cheeks. He never tried to seduce me or be too sexual with me.

In spite of his alleged bad reputation with girls, I found him different from what people thought about him. In the small, enclosed society of Tel Aviv, gossip was a major institution. A lot of people thrived on it. Everyone seemed to have a complete dossier on each other. Mole hills were blown out of all proportion into mountains.

He once showed me the picture of a girl from Aden. At that time, she was living in London. He didn't tell me what his relationship with that girl was, it didn't particularly interest me. My path was to cross with hers in the coming months.

As we grew to like and understand each other more, my music composer suggested we could travel and do concerts, entertaining the Jewish community abroad. The first phase of his plan being that he would go to England, and as soon as practicable, he would send me the necessary papers I would need to join him.

Shortly after he arrived in England, he wrote to me saying that his plans about my joining him would not materialize. Consequently, he had decided to go to Paris. He arranged that I would join him in Paris weeks after he arrived there. I was so excited and flattered by the whole concept of me going to Paris, I felt as though I was walking in a dream and proudly traveled by boat from Haifa to Marcel, then took a train to Paris. Waiting to collect me in Paris was the lady he had shown me in the picture a few months before. She was about twenty-seven years old while I was just a teenager.

The music composer, Nardi, who I came to regard as my coach, introduced her to me as Madlyn. She, also, was a singer, so we formed a trio going to a rehearsal room to rehearse Hebrew and Yiddish songs. We met a Jewish family who helped us in organizing halls and other things we wanted done.

Our first concert in Paris we were welcomed with great approval from the Jewish community there. They threw a party for us where I happened to meet, Chagall, the painter, and his wife. He was very proud to show me a new book that illustrated some of his paintings. He asked me to go to his house whenever I had the time; he would have liked to paint me. I guess that in that time, I did not take him seriously, and besides, I was busy rehearsing and preparing to go to the next concert.

I found out as we worked together, that though Madlyn had a very strong musical disposition, she was not as artistic and talented as I was, but because she was older than I was, she often had the privilege of ending the concerts we did together.

We traveled quite a lot around Paris, but we were not able to break even financially.

Whenever the financial strain got unbearable, my coach normally told me to ask Boubush for some financial assistance, which he offered unhesitantly.

We stayed in a cheap hotel where I shared a double room with Madlyn and my coach.

One night, after we had both gone to bed, I sneaked out of my bed and went to join my coach in his bed. He was not as warm toward me as he used to be when we were in his house in Israel. I wanted him to resuscitate the affection he had once showed me. I lay in his arms while he cuddled and kissed me.

Suddenly, the lights went on. I had thought Madlyn was asleep when I got out of the bed. My coach and I lay on the bed, not knowing what to do. A few minutes later, Madlyn dressed and left the room.

Though we had no sexual relationship, my coach and I were very confused over what had happened. Later, there was a row between Madlyn and me.

We did only two concerts in Paris before we decided to have a change of scene and go to Brussels. We packed our belongings and went to the train station. I was quite upset all the way to Brussels. Madlyn sat with my coach in the same seat while I sat facing them. I cried for hours, but they completely ignored me, as though I was a stranger to them. Throughout the journey from Paris to Brussels, they didn't mention a single word to me. I felt lonely and abandoned, like a dog that had gone astray. My coach, who had been so loving in the past, suddenly turned his back on me as if he did not know me. When we arrived in Brussels, we checked into a hotel which was about a mile from the station.

After we had unpacked, they invited me to go out to look for a restaurant and eat with them, but I declined. I was too upset and not in the mood to go anywhere with them.

While they were out looking for a restaurant, I acted impulsively and decided to part company with them. I am, by nature, a very impulsive person. I do things without seriously considering the implications.

I hurried to the station and bought a return ticket to Paris. I was very nervous, sitting in the train, worrying for the train to leave the station as soon as possible. I was scared that they might come to the station and take me back. I just had to run away, I could not take the pain they had caused me.

When I got to Paris, I telephoned Boubush and told him I wanted to go back to Israel to join the army. I laid a lot of emphasis on the army, because I realized the Jews abroad were very patriotic and often made contributions to help the army. After a long hesitation, he offered to pay my fare to Israel but asked me not to mention it to my music coach, Nardi.

I was pleased and relieved by the fact that I was going back to Israel. My music coach, Nardi, had arranged about ten or twelve concerts in Europe that were supposed to have commenced in Brussels. I knew, without me, those concerts would not take place because Madlyn would not be able to cope on her own.

By leaving them in Brussels, I felt justice had been done. I had paid them back for the emotional torture they made me go through.

A little while after I arrived back in Israel, I gathered my music coach, Nardi, and Madlyn had complained to the police in Brussels about my disappearance. I also learned that they got married. However, their marriage did last a very short time.

I wanted to join the army with the desire to be a member of the entertainment group. Normally, anyone was eligible, as long as one was of Israeli extraction without any obvious disabilities. I was well qualified, you would not find, in those days, anyone my age already performing in concerts, especially abroad. The system was, and it is still, very corrupted in favor of Ashkenazi Jews in Israel and all over the world. They adopted a system of discrimination against Yemenite and Sephardic Jews. They were very repotic and tribalistic. Just because I was a Yemenite girl, those Ashkenazi, who at that time, controlled everything in Israel from the top of the government to all top employees, including the army, refused me. I was not even considered for an audition with all my talents and experience. So, I decided to join the air force. In the air force, we were provided with clothes and with a period of training.

I used to be quite easygoing and at time boisterous. That made me very outstanding amongst the other girls in the army.

Surprisingly, for me, one of my trainers, during the military drill, asked me to go with her. She told me she had arranged for an appointment for me to see a psychiatrist.

Before I could recover from the shock, I found myself interrogated by the psychiatrist. It never ceased to baffle me that being active and jovial could be reasons to see a psychiatrist.

At the end of the session, she said if ever I wanted to leave the air force, she would release me.

CHAPTER SIX

I

I went through the basic army training for two months. Then I was posted to serve the air force by working on the switchboard.

I did not live on the premises of the air force base. I usually took a bus to the base from my grandmother's house, which was not very far away.

Shortly after arriving at the base, I had the occasion to make a request to the commander in charge as to whether I could go for a ride in one of the light aircrafts as a few other people there been granted such a privilege.

After a few days, surprisingly, my request was granted, and he asked me to accompany him and one other senior officer on a twenty minute flight around Tel Aviv. It was my first flying experience, and I enjoyed the sight of the landscape and the beaches, although an aerial view of the city itself revealed that it was very crowded and not well planned. The only problem with the ride was that, during the flight, the changes in the air pressure had an adverse effect on my ears.

The air force had a band which played orchestral music to entertain the senior officers who had special nights when they danced and socialized with each other. I very much wanted to sing with the orchestra, but my earlier upbringing in music had been mainly in the field of Israeli folk songs.

However, I was advised to approach the orchestra conductor and ask if I could sing with him. He was a fat man with a rather protruding belly who wore glasses. I was told that I would find him in Café Nogha, a place where music agents and other show-business people used to communicate in order to get gigs.

I met him one day at Café Nogha at the lunch hour, the place had all the hazel and basal, like a street marketplace where everyone is talking to each other; some are sitting, some are standing or just wandering around. I asked around about him, his name was Mr. Tayaic. He was busy discussing with agents in order to give his army musicians jobs on the side. I made my proposition to him, and told him that I was a singer, which he accepted in principle. However, he was too busy organizing gigs and had many other commitments, so he did not get around to arranging anything for me.

I had several boyfriends, all of whom were civilians. But I had not had intercourse with any of them because I was scared of losing my virginity and the pain such an experience would probably cause me. Come to think of it, I wasn't quite in love with any particular boy in the real sense of the word, but because of the number of boys I was often seen with, I came to have a very bad reputation as a promiscuous girl.

I deliberately changed boyfriends quite frequently because I did not want to be sexually involved, as that may have led to sexual intercourse.

Whenever I went to a beach or public garden with a boy it was inevitable that he would sometimes cuddle and kiss me. The general impression people got was that there must have been a sexual involvement in the relationship.

The beach in Tel Aviv was a focal point and the centre of attraction for quite a number of people, especially at night when the moonlight provided a romantic setting for couples who sometimes liked to swim in the warm Mediterranean water.

When I was eighteen years old, my reputation as a go-go girl who liked to enjoy herself put me in good stead. I mixed very easily with socialites, such as the cream of the show business personalities in a café called Casit. They used it as a rendezvous. The café used to be like a second home to me.

I met a Bohemian man in the café who seemed an easygoing sort of person with a pleasant disposition. He was bearded and about twenty-eight years old. Though I was friendly with him, I didn't particularly love him or think he was something special.

One afternoon, I accepted an invitation from him to go on a ride in his car, which I accepted because I had nothing better to do. I had no idea where we were going, but it didn't bother me in any way. I suppose it was one of my shortcomings to trust people too readily.

As we drove through Tel Aviv, it became apparent to me that we were driving out of town. About half an hour's drive brought us to a ramshackle house which could really pass for a hut. The surroundings indicated that it was not a normal place of residence because it showed neglect.

I felt very strange in the dismal surroundings. Either the place belonged to him, or he had permission to use it from the owner. He invited me into the house where he began to make advances toward me. Half-heartedly, I allowed him to continue to kiss and cuddle me hoping it was going to stay at that, but it didn't stop there. He began to remove my clothes forcibly as I protested that I was a virgin, and that he shouldn't attempt to dishonor me.

As far as he was concerned, gossip had made me out to be an unscrupulous fun-loving girl and talk about being a virgin was a waste of words because he did not believe me or did not care.

His strength was much superior to mine and he succeeded in stripping me. There was little I could do except to try and struggle out of his firm grip. Shouting couldn't have done me any good because the house was built on an isolated strip of land many hundreds of meters from any other house. He forced himself into me and started to rape me violently. I began screaming and yelling for help realizing I was bleeding. He was so engrossed with raping me that he did not heed to my pleas.

Even when he had satisfied himself, he still didn't show signs of believing I wasn't putting on an act, or, perhaps *he* was putting on an act. I had no way to know.

On our way back to town, I was crying at the loss of my virginity. It was a traumatic experience for me.

It took some time before it dawned on him that I was a virgin as I had claimed to be. He apologized for disbelieving me and raping me, but then it did not matter because the deed had been done. I was no longer a virgin.

In a way, with my reputation, it was difficult for him to have taken my word that I was a virgin. On the other hand, what he wanted me to believe, quite apart from my reputation, was that I was a bit overdeveloped for my age. I was eighteen, but I had the physical attributes of a very mature woman.

I told my grandmother about the rape, and she advised me to report it to the police.

I refused to do that, because, to my way of thinking, that would have been tantamount to flogging a dead horse.

II

I never really had any lasting love relationship with any particular person after the loss of my virginity. I once had an affair with a much older man who was about forty years old. He never took me very seriously. He manipulated and used me at will. He also caused me a lot of grief. Once, I found myself lying on the floor of a very dark room. I cannot recapitulate clearly the circumstance that led to it, but I know that after I had been there for quite a few days, my mother appeared on the scene. She leaned over me and asked me to come home with her. My mother had been brought there by the older man I had been going out with. However, what he did not tell her was that he was going out with me.

It later became apparent to me, when my mother took me home, that I was pregnant. My mother was distressed over it, so was the rest of the family. The pride of the family was hurt. It was sacrilegious to get married and not be a virgin. To be pregnant outside matrimony was a sacrilege.

My mother advised me to see a doctor to procure an abortion. The abortion was undertaken at their expense. My mother never mentioned things like the birth control pill. She belonged to the old school who never talked about what to do to prevent a pregnancy.

I was fed up with being in the army after a while. I wanted a career in music, and by remaining in the army, I would not have had the platform to realize that dream.

I spoke to a female lieutenant in the army about my ambition and why I wanted to leave the army. She was very furious with me. She spoke at length about how I had no sense of patriotism and how the society could do without disgruntled elements like me. Her speech was designed to hurt me, but I completely insulated myself from the words of condemnation. The effect it had on me could be likened to the effect a fly would have on a solid brick wall.

As far as I was concerned, I had been a pawn all my life, often used and misused. I was just an unimportant speck in the vast void she called the society. To me, the society had not done anything to improve my lot in life. Except for my music teacher, nobody seemed to have showered any kind of love or affection on me.

I eventually left the army, and I began singing in nightclubs, learning a few songs in English. I met Zigi, a young piano player who I had met toward the end of my career in the army. This young piano player had a lucky break when Oscar Peterson, a notable American jazz pianist, came to Israel performing with Ella Fitzgerald. Oscar Peterson was quite impressed when he heard him play and offered to send him to his private school in New York to train as a better jazz player. Zigi had already come back from America when I met him.

Though the influence of Oscar Peterson was evident in his style of play, Zigi was heavily involved in the Bill Evans style. He became one of the best jazz piano players in all of Europe, if not the best, in my opinion.

We worked together for few months in a couple of nightclubs. I taped most of the stuff I did with him. He must have been only about twenty-two years old. I was very fond of him. Later, that fondness developed into love. I remember I wanted him so much, I once took him to a hotel and paid the bills. I got to know more about him as our intimacy grew. He told me he was born in Poland and came to Israel when he was twelve; the same year he began playing the piano. His father used to chastise him, both physically and verbally, in order to make him play the violin at the age of five. He also told me quite a lot about his family and the secrets of his life.

Through him, I was introduced to smoking Hashish. I smoked it with him as a way of expressing my love to him and show I was ready to adapt to his way of living.

His interest in me began to wane after about three weeks. Musically, he was more ambitious than me. I had a very bad reputation and to be seen too much in my company might have detracted from him as a talented piano player.

Moreover, he thought I was not in the same class with him in the field of entertainment. So, the relationship ended abruptly. He was my first real love. I told my mother how much I cared for and loved him.

After that sad experience, I met a twenty-nine-year-old woman from Haifa who had a Bohemian boyfriend. She had very long, black hair, fair skin, and was very good looking. She was a very bad influence on me. She seemed to have her finger in every pie: prostitution, hostessing, and the like. One day, she told me she was organizing a party for certain journalists whose specialty was writing about the impropriety of those in authority in a magazine called *This World*. They were not interested in the mundane happenings of everyday political life, they basically thrived on scandals. She thought it would be a great idea if I did a striptease for them. She impressed upon me that if I wanted to be famous, this would be the break I had been waiting for.

The idea of a striptease was repulsive to me. Now and again, at that time, some foreign girls from more liberally-minded countries did the odd striptease. But for an Israeli girl, more so, a Yemenite like me, to expose herself in the company of men would be the height of indecency. I told her I did not like the idea, yet I decided I was going to be present at the party to mix with famous people in the entertainment business.

During the course of the party, she persuaded me to be sociable and drink alcohol, which I had never drunk before. She filled my glass each time it was empty until I was drunk. I must have drunk more than half a bottle of whisky. When she thought she had me where she wanted me, she announced to the journalists that I was going to do a striptease.

Although I was drunk, I still had some inhibitions and self-control. I insisted I wasn't going to do it. They starting arguing with me, telling me that I hadn't the guts to do it, and that I was scared stiff. I replied by saying I was not scared. After a protracted argument, during which my resistance was systematically eroded, I ended up agreeing to do it, to prove my ego so to speak.

A St. Louis blues was played, and I went on the stage, stripping to my waist. The crowd cheered and clapped as I danced to the tune of their cajolery and the music. The cameras flashed as my well-developed breasts gyrated. The pictures later appeared in the centre spreads of *This World* with comparisons made with known stars. They caused such a storm that whenever I walked through the streets of Tel Aviv, I was often identified as the girl whose naked body was displayed in the magazine.

I was very embarrassed. My grandmother was particularly angry with me because I used her name as my artistic name. By doing a striptease act, I had ruined and denigrated the name of my family she said.

After that, I did several gigs in clubs. I always felt insulted when people suggested to me I would be fantastic as a stripper rather than a singer, although I was quite talented in the latter.

I had ceased to go out with the young piano player, but I discovered he had impregnated me. I told him about it. He said he did not want a child because he did not see both of us making sense in each other's lives.

Though I wanted to have the child, it had to be born in matrimony, which was something I wasn't going to get into with him. The only alternative open to us was to procure an abortion. He promised to raise the money for the abortion. He only gave me half the amount, the other half I got from my mother. It was my second abortion. The doctor warned me that since I already had one, it would be dangerous if I had a third one.

I decided the best thing was for me to get some contraceptives from a doctor. In my naivety, I had previously thought I could do without them. I never really had any real plans. I lived from day to day. I allowed things to happen to me. I made no real attempt to make things happen my way.

After the abortion, I lived with a drummer who was a friend of Zigi. While I was with him, I learned to sing songs by Billy

Holiday; I was listening to Charlie Parker and other popular musicians at that time. I combined singing with being a hostess. I used to drink myself sick and get depressed because there were no singing jobs. I started to go downhill.

I went out with a middle-aged man who gave me a lot of money. I saved some of this and decided to leave for Paris because I was getting too notorious. I had the address of a French girl, a friend of my sister, Debra. This French girl once lived with my grandmother. I made up my mind I was going to stay at her place.

I traveled by ship from Haifa to Marseille. From there, I took a train to Paris. The French girl met me at the station and took me to her home in a nice, upper-class, residential area. Later on, she told me her mother had committed suicide.

About ten days after my arrival, my sister came from Israel. My sister said she was expecting a Canadian she had met whilst she was picking bananas in the kibbutz. The Canadian was expected to arrive in France through Turkey because it was cheaper that way from Israel.

The three of us went out that night. I had no idea what plan they had. We stopped at someone's private house. My sister and her French girlfriend each found themselves good looking, young French men for the night. I was not in the mood for such things. I remember sitting most of the night in the kitchen, waiting, and trying to have a conversation with a young French man who did not speak English. He wanted to sleep with me and kept pointing out to me that this was what the French girl and my sister were doing in different bedrooms.

A few days after my sister's Canadian boyfriend arrived in Paris, we all went to a discotheque called BILL BOUQUET, not far from Sanja Mar Dupre. After the disco, we fell into conversation. My sister exuded a lot of confidence and gave the impression she felt secure with her boyfriend.

I don't quite know what got into me. I guess a pang of jealousy must have shot through me. In an outburst, I accused her of being unfaithful to her boyfriend. I told him how she was in the habit of going out with other men, but it didn't seem to bother him.

Strangely enough, even after they got married, she lived with a man in Las Vegas for over nine months. He still wanted her back. Marital infidelity did not mean anything to him. A week after he arrived in France, he took my sister to London, England, then to Canada, his home.

I continued to stay with the French girl until her grandmother wanted me to move out of the house. The French girl told me that the house was hers, but her grandmother was the legal guardian until she would be old enough to take control of it. However, one day, they arranged for a car to take me somewhere of my choice to stay. I guess they must have been tired and bored with having me around.

I was checked into a cheap hotel where I paid ten francs a day. It took me a few days to absorb the shock of being asked to leave. I went to the Bill Bouquet disco one night when Johnny Holiday, the French rock singer, was performing. The setting of the discotheque was a sharp contrast with anything Israel had to offer at that time. Around the place were a lot of innocent looking boys and girls. At least, that was how I saw them at that time.

Time, they say, is the enemy of everything. Later, I got to know that most of the so-called innocent-looking boys and girls were homosexuals, queers, gigolos, drug pushers, and prostitutes.

Inside the discotheque, I saw a baby-faced innocent-looking blonde who smiled at me when our eyes met. I smiled back at him. Really, in the state I was in, I was looking for a boyfriend. I joined him where he was sitting. He asked me if I would come home with him. I agreed without any hesitation. He took me to his house where he took me straight to his bedroom. He stripped me and made love to me. After making love, he went into the hallway to make several telephone calls, speaking in French. The telephone calls continued as I lay glassy-eyed on the bed.

I must have slept for a while before I was awakened by the sound of voices. I opened my eyes to find a man I had never seen before walk toward me. I was frightened to death. From another room, I could hear the voice of the blond man who had brought me to the house. I called his name, but he did not answer. A roar of laughter suggested they were in a jocular mood. Grinning from ear to ear, he grabbed me by the shoulders and leant his weight on me. I was in a moribund state. I could not shout, I seemed to have lost my voice.

I was helpless as he raped me. When he had finished, another came in, then yet another. They were six in number. The sixth man appeared to be a very violent man. My tears were flowing like water from a tap as I was screaming. He made jest of me as he raped me by saying my crying meant it must have felt good, what was happening to me.

I was full of self-pity and hatred for the men, especially the blonde man who had brought me to his house. If I had had a gun, I would not have had any compunction about shooting them.

At the break of dawn, I heard the men speak excitedly in French until one of them came in and gesticulated it was time to go. I was mentally saying to myself they would be sorry for what they had done to me. I would go to the police and make a report. We went downstairs through a white, enclosed, narrow staircase and then into a black car. As we drove along, I tried to memorize the names of the streets, but it seemed a futile exercise. I only knew how to read Hebrew which was from right to left. Applying the same principle to the French words made them unintelligible to me. I gave up trying to memorize the street names after a few minutes.

After about three or four miles' drive, they stopped the car outside an underground station and asked me to get out of the car. I felt awful, trashed, and depressed as I walked into the underground station.

I remember thinking to myself what a cruel world it was. Life had no meaning for me. I had nothing to aspire toward. I had no self-respect. The men must have been very mean and unscrupulous.

When I got back to the hotel I was staying at, I overheard someone say there was a cheaper hotel not far away which cost seven francs, three less than I was paying. Since I had no sources of income, and the money I had was running out, I checked out and moved into the new hotel. The room I had in the new hotel was in a ramshackle state. I felt like a horse living in a filthy stable.

Life became a drag for me. I sat idly doing nothing. One day, I was engaged in conversation with a few youngsters who told me they knew a café where I could meet people who didn't speak French, and some English and Americans used it as a rendezvous. Anything was better than idling away in the hotel, so I decided to go to this café. It turned out to be a place where drugs were taken. As the youngsters had said, there were a few English and Americans there. I was introduced to a drug called Mexitone by a group of American youngsters I met there. The Mexitone was dissolved in a glass of water and taken. It was a stimulant that made one feel high and awake in contrast to the effect of hashish which made one sexy. As time went on, my circle of acquaintances widened. In this circle were two American girls who were junkies. One was a model with black, shoulder-length hair, and the other was blonde who wore spectacles. In a conversation that took place in the café one day, they mentioned the fact that the blonde girl's boyfriend would be released from a mental home that day. He had been taken there because of his suicidal tendencies. To celebrate his release, they invited me to an empty house in the company of a painter who I gathered was the blonde's boyfriend. Because there was no furniture in the house, we all sat on the floor. They started injecting themselves with a syringe. I was not a junkie in the real sense of the word. I accompanied them to the house because anywhere I could stay was like a home to me in my homeless state.

I found myself participating with them in their trip to a world of fantasy where the junkie reigned supreme. A rubber band was tied around my arm before I was injected. I became drowsy after a few minutes, and then I must have relapsed into a deep sleep in which my powers of consciousness must have been at their lowest ebb, because I couldn't remember anything that happened. Immediately, my drowsiness engulfed me. When I began to regain consciousness, I felt as if I was lying in a coffin, buried in a shallow grave. I was struggling to get out of the coffin, but I could not muster enough strength and courage. That feeling of utter helplessness persisted for a long time before I relapsed into another deep sleep. When next I opened my eyes, it was well into the afternoon.

I used to pay frequent visits to several jazz clubs, notable among them was one called Blue Knot where famous drummers used to play. In Israel, when I used to mix with musicians and listen to records, Kenny Clarke used to be admired a great deal by musicians and non-musicians alike. Before I left Israel, I met a friend of his who was also a drummer. He told me if ever I ran into him in Paris, I should give him his very deepest regards. When I met him in the jazz club, I told him I was a singer. He asked me to sing something and I sang "Blue Moon," "Summer Time," and "Embraceable You" which were the only English songs I knew then.

The other musicians liked my singing and ridiculed the resident singer there, an American girl who tried to model her style of singing on Billy Holiday and assumed the mannerisms of a whore.

One of the piano players, a French man in the club, wanted to befriend me, but I wasn't interested in him. I met a saxophone player who I took to the Blue Knot quite often. One day, we went to popular club called Bade Cup run by a big, black, American woman who was the wife of the late Bade Powell. A lot of black Americans were always at the club. The music there was of very high quality. They played danceable jazz. I approached the band and told them I could sing. I sang a few songs that impressed everyone. The fat, black, American woman urged me to sing; to put it in her own words, she kept saying, "Sing in Israelite, sing in Israelite." I had a very good backing from the band. The piano player was particularly good. They jazzed every Israeli folk song I sang, and of course, the songs I sang were Nardi compositions that were a combination of Middle Eastern and classical sounds. After I left the stage and sat there with other fellow musicians, they were smoking grass and marijuana, which made the club foul of smoke. The other musicians kept asking me to come outside. In an excited mood, the drummer asked me, "Do you know you made history?" I was wondering what he was trying to tell me, and he said, "Listen to this" as he played the recording he made during the time I was on the stage, singing those Israeli songs. "You were making Israeli jazz." Nobody ever thought of doing that before. With me, it was just natural; I was just singing. It was something new and seemed to have swept them off their feet. All the songs were recorded on cassette.

They advised me to take my music very seriously. That night, the black drummer took us to his house. On the way, we stopped by a bakery; we bought about three dozen hot croissants. We ate and smoked hashish until about four in the morning when we retired to bed.

I used to keep in touch with Boubush in times of trouble, and he sometimes helped me financially.

One day, I received a phone call from a French man who claimed to be a producer and own a record company. He told me to come and meet with him at his recording studio.

At that time, my head, my mind, my being, and my whole existence were above a big sea, floating in a smoke, foul of grays and darkness; I was running away, escaping from myself. I was flying between these clouds with my soul. I just did not know how to take care of myself; no one lectured me about dignity, about the need of education, or about the important need of being ambitious. I had a strange an explainable resistance to anything that came my way, thinking it would harm or hurt me in one way or another. I was frightened by life itself. I could not believe that something good could come my way, so I decided not to take risks reacting negatively to every issue. I did not practically pay any attention or feel excited when the French producer called me; I did not care, it did not enter into my disturbed mind, the question of any future. I did not know the meaning of future.

Entering his office, he showed me his recording studio, were I saw a new grand piano. I felt that all this was a lie, and it was not happening to me. I could not comprehend the idea that someone could be sincerely interested in someone like me who is dirty, homeless, useless, and an ugly creature.

The French producer was short and round; he spoke English. He told me that he wanted to record me, and that he liked my voice. I asked him how he knew that I could sing, he replied that he had heard me, and that he was very impressed. He wanted me to sing in French. "I don't know French," I replied.

"Nevermind, I will teach you to sing in French," he said. "I'm a jazz singer." (I only knew three or four American standard songs at that time, and I was like a stupid young woman bragging about it.) I started to walk away when he shouted at me, asking me to think about it.

On my way out, taking the Metro, I returned to the dirty, cheap motel, not having enough money to pay for that night.

If I was a normal young woman, I would have desperately agreed with the French producer, who had practically offered me a job, and that would have been the best thing that had happen to me. The only thing I had to do was very simple, it was to ask him to provide me with food and accommodation. I was desperate and did not realize the circumstances I was in. I was sure he would have gladly provided for me. We never came as far in our conversation to discuss the financial side of it. Without a manager who would have jumped on the offer, encouraging me to accept it, pushing me to become a professional singer, I was just lost, too blind and timid to understand that here I had the big break of a lifetime, and I was throwing it away.

Instead of a musical career, I become a prostitute to my shame, desperation, misery, lack of money, and of course, lack of knowledge of the French language. I knew very well how to hurt myself without realizing it.

I met a black man who had light skin, freckled, with ginger hair in the Bade Cup nightclub. He told me he came from Detroit. Like him, all his friends were soldiers and belonged to the American bases about twenty miles away from Paris. He was a very vulgar man who was always swearing "shit man" while he was driving with other soldiers. Listening to a French radio, he complained that the French could not sing pop, rock-n-roll, or soul. I went out with him a few times. During one of those times, he took me to the American base, where, for the first time in my life, I had an American hamburger and french fries. I thought that this food was made in heaven. He used to steal boxes of cigarettes from his base and sell them to civilians on the black market.

I slept with him few times in his base, and he had a habit of hitting me. But one day, he hit me so hard, and as always, for no apparent reason, that I ran away and did not want to see him ever again.

During one of my visits to the café Sent, I met a blonde man called Dadley. He was typically English looking, about five foot nine inches tall, slim, and wore glasses. His big, blue eyes made him quite attractive to me. He had a friend with him called Nigel, an averagely built man, not good looking, with broad, thick-rimmed glasses. As we chatted together, Dadley excused himself to go to the toilet. He must have been there for over two hours, it seemed very weird to me that he should spend such a long time in there. However, when he came out, we had some Jambo, my favorite sandwich combine with ham and lettuce on french bread. While we were there, I flirted with him as I hadn't anywhere to live. He told me he did not have a place of his own and that Nigel and he were living with an English friend called Brayen who worked during the day and studied French in the evenings.

Both of them spent a few minutes discussing what Brayen's reaction would be if they took me back to his place. They were only visitors in his place. Nigel seemed to maintain a neutral stance, neither rejecting nor accepting the idea.

In the end, Dadley said he would take me there, but he was not making any promises. The onus of deciding whether I would be able to stay would rest with Brayen, who rented the house. I told Dadley that I was going to share the same bed with him so that Brayen should not be worried about the extra problem of providing accommodation facilities.

We passed the time together. Every now and then, I impressed on Dadley how serious I was in wanting to move in with him in Brayen's place. At about 2:00 a.m., we took a cab to my hotel that was in the centre of Paris and only about twenty-five minutes' drive from the café Sent. I collected my few belongings and gladly checked out of the hotel.

Brayen's house was situated in an industrial area. He didn't seem to mind my moving into his house, so I was quite pleased I had a temporary home.

I spent most of the time with Dadley, chatting and making love to him. Each time I went to bed with him and fell asleep, I always had a ticklish sensation caused by the top of his fingers running over my body. This went on for about three nights. It irritated me, so I had to tell him to stop it. When he denied responsibility for it, I lost my temper with him.

I remember that day in the kitchen; I was preparing something we were all going to eat. Brayen had gone to work, when I began to chastise Dadley verbally in the presence of Nigel about how weird and useless he was. I showered abuses at him. I called him a bum and a piece of garbage. He just stared at me without saying anything. I told him to sit in the bin by the corner of the kitchen. To my surprise, he obeyed.

He was there for quite a while until Nigel could no longer bear what was happening. He pleaded on Dadley's behalf before I asked him to get up.

Whenever Brayen went to work, we always loused around the house smoking Hashish and not doing anything productive. Dadley and Nigel began to get on my nerves.

I decided I was going to convince Brayen to get rid of them. I pointed out to him that they were parasites and bums who were taking advantage of him, not contributing anything toward the food expenses and rent.

Brayen was not hard to convince. His attitude toward Dadley and Nigel changed. He later told them that they had to move out of his house.

A few days after that, they left the house and later returned to England.

I continued to live in Brayen's house after their departure. I decided to clean the house which was in a messy state. Brayen had a pile of dirty clothes, which was about four feet high from the floor. Some of the underwear on the pile were fairly new, but they had excrement in them. I used to wonder how he could stand living in so much filth. He really looked wild. He had long black hair growing out of his nostrils to his upper lip. I asked him to trim it. I helped him look decent and sophisticated in appearance.

CHAPTER SEVEN

I

Shortly after Dadley and Nigel left Brayen's house, I noticed the ginger-haired black American I used to go out with come to the premises and peep through the window. He did this on about three of four occasions. Each time, I was frightened. I was glad when he finally stopped hanging around outside the premises.

Living in the same house with Brayen, I guess it was only a matter of time before the inevitable happened. One night, I went to bed with him. He told me it was his first sexual experience as he had never had a girlfriend before, although I reckoned he was about twenty-two or twenty-three years old, which would have made him about three years older than me.

After about three or four weeks, I discovered I was pregnant. The pregnancy must have been about two or three months along. I had no illusion of who was responsible for it. I knew it was not Brayen. It had to be Dadley. I remember vividly the first time he went to bed with me. I told him to be careful and not to ejaculate inside me, but he ignored the precaution and finished inside me. I remember thinking to myself he was not a very reliable person. He should have been more careful. At that time, I had run out of the contraceptive pills I had brought with me from Israel. I couldn't get any from the chemist because a prescription from a doctor was needed for that purpose, and I couldn't afford the consultation fee to see one.

So, I decided I was going to be careful as far as sex was concerned, hence my precaution to Dadley. It never, for any moment, crossed my mind that the American black man with the ginger hair I had gone out with could have been responsible for the pregnancy. I had no iota of doubt about it not being Dadley's baby.

Brayen also knew he was not responsible for it, so I decided I was going to have an abortion. I couldn't have a child without getting married by Israeli tradition. Unlike Israel, where abortions were relatively cheap, it was expensive in Paris. Brayen had no money to foot the bill, but we gathered, somehow, that there was a woman who could do it for a very nominal fee, but her method was very unconventional. She did it in the bath with her own tools. I thought it would be too dangerous to go to this woman because of the possibility of anything going wrong, since she was not qualified to do it legally. Besides, I had done it twice before, and on the last occasion, I was warned by the doctor that I might jeopardize my life if I did it again.

I decided, if I was going to have an abortion, it had to be done by a specialist. So I went to a Jewish friend called Boubush, whom I first met when I was singing with Nardi and Madlyn. I asked him to help me meet the financial commitment entailed in having an abortion. He was a very rich man by any stretch of the imagination. He had two electrical shops to prove it.

On this occasion, he did not want to help me. He made reference to the fact that he sometimes gave me money to pay my hotel bills when I couldn't afford it, and he wasn't going to continue to give me any financial help.

Each time he gave me some money, he always wanted me to pay him back sexually, but he was not capable of having a sexual affair. He always wanted me to play around with his little penis. Because I was not keen on doing that, I guess he became frustrated, hence the withdrawal of any financial assistance.

I was very disappointed over his failure to help me.

Since I could not raise the money for the abortion from anywhere else, I decided to convince Brayen to go to England in search of Dadley.

After about three weeks, Brayen left Paris bound for England in search of Dadley. When he left, I wasn't feeling very well. My main diet consisted of biscuits, which I ate and vomited day after day. It was a gruesome experience for me, staying day and night in the attic upstairs, wondering if Brayen would find Dadley.

After about a week, Brayen returned to Paris. He could not find Dadley.

The whole thing was bogging me down emotionally. I had to see him about the pregnancy. I kept on nagging Brayen that he had to go back to England again in search of him, and this time, he should be thorough in his search.

Brayen traveled to England again. After a few days, he came back with the news that Dadley would be coming to see me in Paris in a couple of weeks. A couple of weeks passed, but Dadley did not show up. As the weeks turned into months, I was just living in hope that he would show up.

When I was about six months pregnant, the state of my health improved tremendously. I ceased to be very sick as I was during the early months.

One day, I accompanied Brayen to see an English couple who were his friends. They lived in the Latin quarters; they were intellectuals. While we were there, Brayen had asked the lady to cut his hair for him. She ignored him and started to make jest of him, hovering around his legs and playing very funny and embarrassing games at his expense. I became annoyed so I told her that as long as I was going out with Brayen, I would not sit down anywhere and watch someone take the mickey out of him. In a few words, I asked her to stop the foolery. Her attitude toward Brayen changed immediately after I had told her off.

On our way home, I told Brayen that he should learn to be confident in himself as a man, and he should not allow people to ride roughshod over him. I reassured him that as long as I was with him, nobody would dare insult him without having to contend with me first.

We both went out to the cinema one day during my seventh month of pregnancy. On our way back, as we approached the house, it was apparent that someone had let himself into the house by tampering with the lock, because we had the keys in our possession.

We were quite relieved on entering the house to find it was Dadley. He had with him an ill-matched couple whose manners left much to be desired. They had forced their way into the house. Dadley introduced the man as John Gavel and the woman with him as his wife.

I was ecstatic with joy over the fact that Dadley showed up at last. As we chatted in the sitting room, John Gavel waged a persistent battle of words on his wife, who was just sat there taking everything that was literally thrown at her. He shouted at her, scorned her, and attacked her very aggressively. I believe he was a sadist, while his wife was masochistic. They had to be, to do what they did.

Dadley remained silent as his friend lashed out at his wife. Later, it was established that Dadley had had an affair with John Gavel's wife. When Dadley left France for England, after Brayen told him to leave his house, he had stayed with John Gavel and his wife in Kent, a small town in England, and it was there that their affair started. I believe that he was so hooked on her that was why it had taken him several months to show up in Paris.

The next day, after Dadley's arrival, he started to mock me about how fat and unglamorous I had become. He lifted my breasts up and down and complained that they were too big. He also complained about the size of my tummy. I reminded him that I was pregnant and was not supposed to be a glamour queen. By his words and deeds, it was clear that Dadley did not like me anymore.

At the end of the third day, following their arrival, John Gavel and his wife had succeeded through their wrangling and quarrelling in depressing everyone.

I had no choice but to tell Brayen to ask them to go. Dadley was not interested in the pregnancy, so he left for England with John Gavel and his wife.

My worries were confounded by the fact that, in a few months, I would be a mother, and my child would not have a father whose name he would bear.

There was very little I could do to ameliorate my predicament, so I decided to have a chat with Brayen. I told him I couldn't see myself having a baby without marriage. It was sacrilegious. So I asked him to marry me. It must have been a difficult step to take because he knew I was pregnant by someone else, however, he agreed to marry me.

I told him that there was no future for both of us in France, so we discussed the idea of going back to England. I told him he should take me to the British Embassy so that I could get the necessary papers to go to England with him.

I was refused a visa on the grounds that I had no money. The only way to get around the problem of getting a visa would be to get married, so I decided to apply for a marriage license.

We had a medical check up and presented ourselves in a marriage bureau where the marriage ceremony took place. The marriage vow was read out, culminating in the question as to whether or not I would marry him, I answered in the affirmative. They read out the vow again and asked Brayen the same question. Brayen looked nervous, so I answered in the affirmative for him. He echoed the answer after me. Only two friends of ours were present at the wedding, an Italian called Mario and another friend called Melvin.

After the ceremony, the four of us went into a nearby coffee house to celebrate with a bottle of wine.

My spoken English was not so good. I used to gesticulate a lot because Brayen could not speak Hebrew. I suppose I learned most of my English from him by virtue of the fact that he was always speaking English to me.

A few days after the marriage, we arranged to go to the British Embassy with our marriage certificate to enable me to get a visa to go to England. This time, the visa officer blushed when he recognized me. He said because I was married to an Englishman, I was entitled to have it. So, he issued me an emergency traveling certificate and asked me to apply for a British passport when I arrived in England. Brayen and I were both laughing as we left the embassy. He said he had to inform his mother about the marriage and our plans to come to England. Having done that, we packed our things and got ready to leave France.

II

My husband and I traveled by train from Paris to London. As we embarked on the journey, I was glad to leave France. After the rape and the hard times I had experienced there, I hated Paris. Although I had no idea what coming to London would offer me, somehow I had great expectations about it.

I recalled my first attempt to come to England was through my piano coach, Nardi, but through unfortunate circumstances, it came to a sad fruition.

Although Brayen had written home to his parents about our marriage and date of arrival in London, I was a bit apprehensive about the kind of reception I would receive from them. Brayen's father was from Yorkshire, whilst his mother was Scottish from Glasgow.

On arrival at Victoria Station in London, we were met by Brayen's father, a very warm man who appeared to like me as a daughter-in-law. He drove us in his car to New Eltham, where they had the family home. The house looked unlike what I had been used to in France. It was semi-detached, typically English looking, with a nice garden. Inside, it was exquisitely decorated with velvet curtains and matching furniture. It was my idea of a home.

Our arrival, I believe, was not quite the happy event my mother-in-law had anticipated. It was clear from her reaction when she saw me that her son had not mentioned the fact that I was pregnant. She did not openly express her views about the pregnancy, but her general attitude suggested she probably discussed it with her son.

Our fist meal there was supper, which was comprised of roast chicken and potatoes, apple pie, and some wine. I became introduced to the English way of life. Apart from English meals like roast pork, puddings, pieces of veal, boiled potatoes, and the like, I learned the right way to set a table, and the general table manners that the English cherish very dearly.

My state of health was very good. I ate well and became more physically fit in my last month of pregnancy.

It was plain from my mother-in-law's words and deeds that she disliked me. My father-in-law was a much kinder man who I got along with very well. Maybe some of her hostility toward me stemmed from this fact.

Brayen's younger brother tried to give me some English lessons to improve my English, but I did not take it very seriously. I had a few lessons with him, but they were not enough to make any marked improvement.

I enrolled in a family planning class where I was prepared both physically, by way of exercise, and mentally for the actual delivery of my baby. I attended theses sessions about three or four times a week. My husband's parents discussed with us several possible names to give the child. They also bought a pram, baby clothes, and all the paraphernalia the baby would need.

One day, my husband and I went out on an outing to Woolwich. On our way back, we went to a cinema. As we were coming home from the cinema, I started to feel very uncomfortable. I had an irresistible urge to urinate. Since we were walking together in the street, I tried to restrain myself, but the urge increased. I held my husband's hand for support as we walked along, until I could bear it no longer. I went to a nearby tree where I bent down to ease myself. It seemed to go on for an unusually long time which slightly frightened me. I hadn't the faintest idea what was happening to me. By the time we got home, my pants were completely wet. I told my husband's parents what had happened to me, and they asked me to go upstairs into the bedroom and lie down.

I began to feel better as I lay on the bed, but I noticed I had wet it as well. The best line of action, I thought, would be to go to the hospital, so I told my husband to ring for an ambulance.

He went downstairs in an attempt to call for an ambulance, but his mother stopped him and told him that there was nothing wrong with me. I was merely imaging things, and, according to her, the time of my delivery was still sometime to come. My husband came upstairs to tell me what had transpired between him and his mother. I told him that since I was the person having the baby, I insisted an ambulance be brought to take me to the hospital.

After a few minutes, we had a row with his mother until she conceded and let Brayen phone for an ambulance. When the ambulance did arrive, they put a blanket around me and carried me inside. My husband went into the ambulance with me to a hospital in Woolwich. I was shaved all over my vagina and asked to urinate. My bowels were also cleared to ensure and facilitate the delivery of the baby. As I went through the preparations for the delivery, I was filled with mixed feelings. I was nervous and a bit frightened on the one hand, and happy on the other, because I was going to deliver the baby and would be myself again. There was always this ever-present feeling throughout the pregnancy that I was carrying, not only my weight, but also someone else's.

I was taken to the delivery by the nurses who lifted my legs as I lay on the bed and performed some examinations. They said if I felt any pain I should ring the bell by my bed. I told them I was very frightened and apprehensive. I was injected, presumably to calm me down. After about two hours, I pressed the bell as I started to experience some pain. The nurses came in and gave me some gas which was administered through a mask. I inhaled the gas about twice before the pain started again. They asked me to push. I had no idea how long I pushed. As I lay there, writhing in pain, my husband was brought in putting on a pair of white overalls. I continued to push for a while until the baby's head came out. The rest of the body came out relatively easier. It was a baby boy.

I watched the nurses as they cut the umbilical cord, after which, they inverted the baby, holding onto its legs and smacking its backside. He responded by letting out a yell. They lay him on the table where I am not sure how the baby was being cleaned or washed. I was taken to my room where I lay down. After about a couple of hours, a nurse came in with the baby clad in white. She put the baby in my arms, smiled at me, and left. I was very weak and stared at my son rather curiously. The thought, "Where the hell did you come from," came into my mind. Simultaneously, as if aware of my thoughts, the baby suddenly started crying. That incident stands out very clearly in my mind.

I was in some considerable pain when I tried to breastfeed him because my breasts were slightly inflamed, and the breast milk did not come out very easily in the beginning, but after a while, it became alright.

I went back home after four days in the hospital. Though my husband's parents were Christians, the baby was not taken to church or baptized according to the Christian practice.

We named the baby Jerom, which was one of the names we had chosen earlier, before its birth, which, incidentally, was the name of my grandfather from my father's side.

The first few days after I came out of hospital, we spent resting and taking care of Jerom. After those few days of grace, I began to do all the domestic work. They expected me to prepare the ingredients for the cooking, wash the dishes when everyone had finished eating, and do any odd jobs around the house that needed doing.

A few days later, I asked my mother-in-law where Brayen had gone to. She replied by saying he had accompanied his father to Woolwich to register Jerom as Jerom Hatchett. A pang of conscience went through me as she said that. Later, they returned with his birth certificate.

My relationship with my mother-in-law went from bad to worse. I didn't really know what she wanted from me. The fact that she used me domestically like a slave did not improve our relationship in any way. One day, there was a drama in the house, which was provoked by some trivial thing. She shouted at me saying, "We don't really get on, do we?"

I replied by saying, "You may not get on very well with me, but I know I am alright, there is nothing the matter with me.".

As these bickerings continued, Brayen started getting annoyed. He started considering moving out of the house so that we could live on our own. He was contributing to the rent and food in his parent's house anyway, so it wasn't that we were living there under their charity.

My mother-in-law was racist. Brayen once told me that she had told him never to marry a Jewess. She once knew a Jewish family back in Scotland who she believed was very dirty. She probably thought that all Jews must be like them. She was always grumbling over the fact that I had no education. I used to ignore her whenever she said such things.

She was also in the habit of pushing her husband forward to fight her domestic fights for her. Occasionally, when he was pushed into saying something, he would not otherwise have said, he would remark by saying it didn't really come from him, it was his wife's idea.

The general condition of our relationship was such that it would have been impossible to continue to live there. Brayen began to look in earnest for a place of our own where we could live in peace.

III

After a few weeks' persistent search for a place to live, we were rewarded when Brayen found a large room with a terrace in Archway, North London. Our landlord was a youngish looking man with a red beard who charged us exorbitantly for the room. For that reason, we didn't like him very much.

Apart from the rather high rent, we were quite happy in our new home after we fully settled in.

A few months after the delivery of Jerom, my mother wrote to me asking me to have him circumcised. I asked Brayen to find me a rabbi to perform the ceremony. A few days later, he found one in Golden Green, a Jewish area. Jerom was all ready three months old.

Brayen used to work in the telephone exchange, which was a government job. During the day, when he had gone to work, I spent most of my time at home taking care of Jerom. Opposite the house, lived a group of black musicians. I used to watch them load their musical instruments into vans. One day, I approached the band leader and told him I could sing, but he didn't seem to be interested in me musically. A few months later, the band hit the big time and became famous.

Once, I met the band leader in Denmark Street, which is to musicians what Fleet Street is to journalists. On that occasion, he was surrounded by a bevy of beautiful girls. I wondered if he still remembered me.

I had a friend who lived about three houses away from where I lived. Her name was Suzzane; she was about twenty-three years old. She was half-English and half-Indian. She was very attractive and worked as a hostess in a club, although she told me I shouldn't tell anyone about it. I suspect she didn't want her boyfriend, who lived with her, to know about it. Once, she suggested to me that I apply for a job as a hostess, but I declined because I had to take care of my son, Jerom.

After living in the archway area for about a year, we moved into a better flat in the Notting Hill Gate/Ladbroke Grove area of London. The flat was very close to Portobello Market and was comprised of two bedrooms, one of them very large, a kitchen, and a bathroom. The flat was an unfurnished company let. The house was a Victorian style one. We had a key and access to a very large garden which we shared with our neighbors and the other residents of the houses on the other side of the garden.

Since the house was unfurnished, I bought cheap, second-hand furniture, used velvet curtains, and did a few decorations.

We registered Jerom in a nursery close by after we settled fully in the area. We were financially poor. Brayen had to work overtime quite regularly to enable us to pay the bills.

At times, I used to go to the bingo to gamble, but I do not think I ever won anything substantial. That was a very selfish habit of me. Remembering my life at that time,

I did not take any step to help Brayen or improve myself via education or taking my musical abilities seriously. I was young then, and I had strong, deep, hidden talents.

Living below our flat on the first floor was a young English woman called Mary. She had three children, two from one boyfriend and one from another. She was about twenty-five years old and very friendly. She had quite a big flat which included the ground floor and basement. We used to go out on shopping sprees together.

In order to make ends meet, I got myself involved in several things. I met a woman who wanted to manage me as a singer. She was a middle-aged woman who had a friend who ran an agency for musicians. She wanted to model on Carmen Maranda. She used to have an act where she had a lot of fruits on her hat. She wanted to try it out on me. I felt it was a very cheap way of building me up. Apart from this act, I found her ideas very old fashioned. Once, she arranged that I work out an act with a homosexual. It wasn't quite my scene.

Also in her employment, were two housewives who worked part-time writing songs for her which they wanted me to sing for her. The songs were not very good, so I tried to get myself out of it.

I once participated in a charity show for Jewish children in the Royal Garden Hotel in the West End. I understood more than three hundred thousand pounds was reached from the show.

I did a bit of cabaret in several clubs and tours for about eighteen to twenty weeks. I didn't really enjoy it because I was not well-organized, and, more often than not, my audience was not the cream of the society. I managed to earn a few pounds from it, but I had to give it up because it meant I was away quite a lot from home, and Brayen could not take care of Jerom properly. So, in a manner of speaking, I let it slip through my fingers. I tried to look for work around London but to no avail.

I used to see a few musicians playing near Portobello Market and collecting money. At times, I used to give them a hand, collecting stray coins. I also used to sing some simple Israeli songs. There were times I brought a few of the musician's home. We did some songs together. It wasn't really anything professional; it was more of a hobby.

My husband, Brayen, also tried to help me. He took a few of my photographs around trying to get me a job as a singer.

I remember an agent once told me that they were looking for the kind of image of the girl next door-whatever that was supposed to mean.

I had a quite large circle of acquaintances but no real friends. I wasn't making any headway as a singer either, because I was too lazy and not pulling my weight enough, or

I hadn't anyone to manage me properly and build me up as a good singer. Left on my own, I could not produce anything noteworthy.

Since I couldn't get any singing jobs, I started looking for other jobs.

One day, I saw the job of a hostess advertised in a newspaper. I applied and got the job. It was an easy way of getting money. I was supposed to sing around in the club, waiting for the male clientele to come and buy me drinks. This was a way of making them spend money in the club. I was not very discrete about how I conducted myself. Occasionally, I would go with a customer. The kind of money I got from them was usually what my husband would give me for food for about three weeks.

One day, I told him I had slept with another man, and that he had given me money. I expected some form of reaction from him, but he was silent. I thought he did not care for what I was doing.

I did it quite a few times until word reached the management that I used to tell the customers that they should spend their money on me rather than on buying drinks in the club. I was caught and fired from the job.

CHAPTER EIGHT

I

One day, in the summer of 1969, I impulsively went to a hairdresser and asked how I could change the color of my hair from black to blonde. The hairdresser said it was going to be a difficult job because my hair was very black and would have to be treated with bleach mixed with hydrogen peroxide. It wasn't a very pleasant experience. I had a burning sensation in the roots of my hair as I went through the treatment. After about an hour, the hair turned to pale yellow before it was toned to golden blonde. It transformed my image quite remarkably. I liked it very much. People used to comment about my blonde hair which was accentuated by the fact that they thought my brown complexion was a sun tan. Little did they know that I was not a natural blonde.

After about three weeks, the blackness of the regrowth was so obvious that my hair didn't look nice. So, to keep up with my new image, I went to Selfridge's, one of the biggest shops in London and bought an ash blonde wig which was the nearest color to what I had. The whole gimmick lasted for about two or three months before I reverted back to my natural hair color.

However, before I had gone out one night with the ash blonde wig on, an estate car stopped in front of me. A Jewish man, about thirty-five, who introduced himself as Michael, invited me into the car. At that time of my life, it was nothing new for me to get into a car with a complete stranger.

I told him I was not what he thought I was, and that I was a singer, although not a successful one. I think in an attempt to show off, he told me he was very well off, and that his father owned a glass factory. As an old saying goes, "every door is a door of opportunity," so I decided to tell him about myself. I told him I wasn't making any progress in my career because I hadn't a manager or someone to help and guide me. He replied by saying that he was going to help me. I think he said that, not because he thought I had talent, but because he fancied me as a woman.

Afterwards, when I was leaving his car, he gave me twenty pounds for the pleasure of my company and reiterated that he would like to cultivate my acquaintance so that he could help me.

A few days later, I met Michael again. I told him I had once gone to a music publisher called Cambell and Connolly, and they had shown some slight interest in me as an artist. Maybe if I tried them again, they could renew that interest in me, and if we were lucky, we could work something out together.

He seemed to go along with the idea, so I made an appointment with the publishers to see them.

On the day of the appointment, I went to Denmark Street where they had their publishing office. I spoke to a blonde man of about twenty-three; his name was John Aston. He worked in the engineering and producing side of the company. I let him hear some of the demos I had made previously which I had taken along with me. He liked them very much. I further told him that I knew someone who may be able to finance me in making a single record. Upon hearing that, he was very enthusiastic. He told me that the most important thing is to find a very good song. He let me listen to a few songs that they had for publishing. After a while, he chose a song called "Lazy," which he thought would be very commercial. I told him for me to make it as a singer, I had to have a hit record.

He replied optimistically by saying, "We'll see." I arranged an appointment with him so that Michael, whom I now considered my manager, and I, could meet him. When he met Michael, he opined that with his song and my voice he was confident we would be able to make it. It was going to cost us 100 pounds to make the record in a four track studio. That was in 1969. So, we signed a contract with him. He also signed me on two of my songs which I had personally written, although nothing came out of them.

The way things were going, it appeared I would have to have a sexual relationship with Michael in order to sustain and consolidate the business side of the relationship. I was not in love with him and didn't take him seriously because he was married. And more so, he was the kind of man who had a lot of women on the side. It would have been impossible to have a serious relationship with him.

My husband was not a very intelligent man, he was weak and passive. I was the boss of the house. I helped to restore in him the confidence I think he needed as a man. The humiliating experience he had in Paris at the hands of his friends in the

Latin Quarters was an indication of how low his ego and self-esteem was. In my subconscious mind lay the thought that it was my duty to make a man out of him.

Although he knew that Michael was my manager, my husband paid little more than a passing interest in what we did. In many ways, he was a very weird man. I remember one day, I was walking with him in Portobello Market. We went into a second-hand shop where a long-sleeved jacket made of beads caught my eye. Obviously, because of the fact that the jacket was made of beads, one had to wear it on top of a dress to conceal one's nakedness. I asked him if he could buy the jacket for me. He said he would, on one condition, and the condition was, if I agreed to put on the jacket without any kind of underwear or something inside it. I was shy and taken back at his suggestion. At that time, nobody went around exposing himself or herself that way.

My husband was an exhibitionist. No normal husband would encourage a wife to go around a market half-naked.

With him, there was no act of indiscretion in anything I did. I was at liberty to do anything I wanted.

Once, I was walking down Oxford Street when I spotted a guitarist called Emil whom I knew in Israel. I talked to him in Hebrew and asked him about what he was doing in London. He said he was not doing anything in particular, and he had no place to live. I said he could come and stay with me. My husband did not inquire or object about him when he saw him.

I treated Emil very nicely. A few days after he arrived there, we were reminiscing about events in Israel. I mentioned something about Zigi, the piano player who had impregnated me and helped me procure an abortion. Emil told me that he died of cancer. The news was so shocking that it was hard for me to absorb. I told Emil he should not joke about things like death, there were other subjects where he could do that.

He went on to narrate the circumstances that had led to his death. According to him, about a year after I left Israel, he was so involved in drugs that he stopped playing the piano in spite the fact that he was very talented and could easily have ranked as one of the best in the world. His health deteriorated as a result of a stomach cancer. His stomach became very swollen. Oblivious of his precarious state of health, he believed he was going to be around for a very long time until he was an old man. One day, he gave up the ghost. He was the only child his parents had. Looking back at my life at that time, how much I loved the young man, I wished I had kept his baby, even if it would have been an illegitimate child. It took some time before I resigned myself to accepting the fact that he was dead.

I recall when I was in Paris, I sometimes thought about him. I wrote two letters to him which he did not reply to. I had always nursed a secret desire inside me that if, one day, I made it as a big star, I would go back to Israel and show him that in spite of everything that happened to me, I was a lady.

One day, unaware of the fact that Emil was in the toilet, I opened the door to find him injecting himself with heroin. Although, I used to take soft drugs, I had an argument about it with him. He was so annoyed about it that he told me in the presence of my husband that he could not comprehend why my husband had married me. According to him, I was worthless. He told my husband that everyone in Israel, including him, made love to me. He thought he could shock my husband with anything he said. Brayen just starred at him nonchalantly.

I was amazed at how ungrateful he could be. I told him I had brought him into my house, fed him, and treated him well. He was paying me back for my kindness by defaming my character and trying to ruin my marriage by suggesting to my husband that he made a mistake marrying me. I was so upset I told him to leave the house.

After a couple of weeks, following the signing of the contract, we were ready for the final stages of the recording of the song "Lazy," which would be on the A side, and "That's When I Cry" which would be on the B side.

At the last minute before the recording, John Aston, the producer, suddenly decided to participate in the signing. He was so optimistic about how commercial the song would be that he had dreams of becoming a great star.

I was surprised when I saw him singing with me. We hired a photographer to take pictures of me for the purpose of promotion. A few snapshots were taken on the Cutty Shark and the columns outside the museum in Woolwich.

When the record was released, the publisher managed to get it played on "What's New," a BBC Radio One Lunchtime program. The record was criticized as a bad production. I was interviewed on Radio One about the record, and that was the end of the venture. The record didn't sell.

Because of the commercial failure of the record, I approached the managing director of the publishing company, a balding and ugly man, probably in his fifties, about trying to do another one at the expense of the company.

He had a very imposing office with a grand piano where the pictures of his family were displayed. He said if I could collaborate with him sexually, he would see what he could do for me. He cajoled me into sucking his penis, but he didn't try to do anything for me as he promised. I felt angry that the old man had the nerve to use me the way he did. That incident reminded me of a similar experience I had in Israel, when I was in the army, at the hands of Shacee Sayse, a famous French singer.

It must have been in 1964. As a singer, he was famous in Israel. He gave several concerts there. During one of those concerts, I spoke to a few acquaintances of mine who were musicians about the possibility of meeting him and telling him I sang Israeli songs. I had that childlike longing to meet a famous star. Somehow, someone contacted me and told me that Shacee Sayse was staying in the Hilton Hotel and that he was expecting me. He gave me the room number and insisted I must go there in my army uniform. I did as I had been told and went to the hotel. I knocked on the door and a voice asked me to come in. I went in. Shacee Sayse was lying on the bed. He asked me to sit on the bed. I was amazed and overwhelmed by the presence of such a great star. On the floor in front of the wardrobe, he had an incredible collection of the same sneakers but with different colors.

He asked me if I spoke English, and I said no. He unzipped his pants and removed his penis, and then he asked me to hold it. I was so frightened and confused, shy and so naïve; that was the last thing I thought that would happen to me from such a big star like him. I obeyed. As I did that, he placed his hand on the back of my head and forced it down onto his penis, putting it inside my mouth. My nausea was increased when he actually emitted his sperm inside my mouth. After he had done that, he told me to leave because he had to attend several interviews. I was filled with disgust as I left the hotel. The next day, I went back to the hotel, and he pretended he had never seen me before. I wondered why and who the person was that put me in that situation. I had been used as a sacrificial lamb for Shacee Sayse's sexual fantasies. Since then, I have hated the man.

It remains a mystery to me who arranged the meeting between Shacee Sayse and me and how much money he made out of it. I think he must have got a kick out of having a female soldier suck his private parts. That is why he asked me to go there in uniform.

I was so ashamed and embarrassed over the whole incident that I did not mention it to anyone. Each time I see him on television, I feel sick. The mere sight of him makes me want to puke. I hate him so much that I don't consider him a decent human being. I cannot bear to stare at the evil glint in his eyes, his admirers and audiences do not see behind his make-up.

I remember telling my son when he was fourteen about my experience with him. My son was equally disgusted at him observing "how ratty and false he was with his caterpillar eyebrows," to use my son's description of him.

II

One night, while I was lying on the bed with my husband, some strange thoughts started coming into my mind. The thoughts revolved around how I could avenge my father for the wrongs he perpetrated on me. I said to my husband, "Brayen, do you know what I would like to do to my father?" I went on to narrate to him the train of my thoughts.

"I would like to hire a few gangsters to fly to Israel, kidnap my father, and bring him back to this country in a sack or something. Before then, I would have prepared a hut in a distant, isolated spot somewhere in the countryside, many miles away from anybody. The hut would be his home. His arms and legs would be in chains so that any attempts by him to escape would be foiled. He would be fed with dog food to degrade him and bring him to the level of an animal. Twice or three times per a week bottles would be stuffed inside his rectum.

After that sequence of events, in my thought process came a very brief one. I could hire an assassin who would go to Israel and have him shot in the street, because, in my opinion, he did not deserve to live within the community of decent people. He should not be the recipient of any kind of respect and honor, because he was not worthy of them.

My husband thought my ideas were very good ones.

These kinds of thoughts of mine were projections of the vengeful part of me, but in reality, I doubt if I would have the guts to do them even if I had the potentialities and opportunities.

One thing I had the guts to do was to get rid of a complex I had that had its roots in my father. Right from my childhood, people had always remarked, especially my paternal relations, how similar my nose was with that of my father. Each time I looked into a mirror, that fact always registered itself in my mind, and the thought brought with it a series of thoughts and recollections I would otherwise be glad to be rid of.

I was so bent on doing something about it that I saw my family doctor about the possibility of having an operation. My family doctor said he could not do it himself, so he recommended me to a nose specialist in Harley Street. When the specialist examined me, he said I had adenoids which impaired my breathing, and that he could perform an operation to remove them, and at the same time, do a plastic surgery to alter the shape of my nose. He said it was going to cost two hundred guineas to have both operations done.

When I got home, it occurred to me that since part of the operation was not merely cosmetic to alter my looks but to treat my adenoids, I could have it done under the National Health Service.

I told my husband about my thoughts, and between us, we decided to write a carefully worded letter to the specialist about having the operation done under the National Health Service. He replied by saying it would be possible, but it was going to take about a year before it would be undertaken. I was very impatient and could not wait a year, so I decided to have it done privately. I took up a job as a hostess and raised half of the cost while my husband contributed the other half.

I did the operation, and I think I managed to get rid of that complex because it altered my looks, but I realized from the beauty point of view, the operation was a bad job. I had it redone in Switzerland a few years later.

My stepmother once told me a story, involving my sister, Debra. As a little child, Debra saw our father only a few times, but when she had reached an age when she could exercise her powers of cognition and memory, she never saw him. When she was a fully-grown adult, already married with two children, she used to like to fool around with other men. When she went to Israel for few months to visit, it was unique in more senses than one. It was, in manner of speaking, Debra's first meeting with our father. She had gone there with a casual lover of hers, whom she introduced to him as her husband. Our father accorded her and her supposed husband the respect that was due to a married couple and showered them with hospitality. My stepmother mentioned to me that she even given her clean sheets for them to spend the night there. However, it transpired that someone who knew what Debra's relationship was with the man, told my father that she was living immorally with him.

My father and my stepmother felt very embarrassed, and my stepmother was very angry and said that Debra would not receive a penny from any inheritance. She was mad at the way Debra had treated them in bringing a lover to the house and lying that he was her husband.

Years later, when I saw Debra, she told me that she did what she did to my father because of the spite she felt toward him. It was an open secret that she did not have an iota of respect for him. This is partly because she knew everything that happened between me and our father when I was a child.

III

Following the demises of my hopes to make it musically through Campbell and Connelly, the music publishers, I began to toy with the idea of getting a band together.

I talked to Michael, my manager, about it, and he said that I should try it out, and if I could get something together, he would try and help. Everything depended on how good the band was. I suppose his interest in me was waning because the novelty and excitement of our sexual relationship had worn off.

I advertised in the *Melody Maker*, a London newspaper, for musicians who were interested in forming a band. A few musicians turned up for the audition. One of them was a bass player called Tex. He was English, aged about twenty-seven, with blue eyes and long, straight, black hair. He was very good looking. He told me he had played bass with a few famous bands including The Blue Not, and when I heard him play, I thought he was very talented. I asked him to help me audition the other musicians, although there were not many to choose from.

We managed to get a group together, and we "jammed" together (to use a phrase from the music world). Anyone who had any bright ideas told the rest of us about it, and we all tried it out.

As we began to know each other better, I found myself fancying Tex. I believe the feeling was mutual. Each time we jammed together, the musicians brought hashish and marijuana, which we smoked together.

Tex was heavily involved in drugs. The pills he gave me were completely new to me. One day, I went to his house with the keyboard player. During my next visit to his place, I slept with him.

During that period, my relationship with my husband deteriorated progressively. We got on each other's nerves and didn't see eye-to-eye in most things. We argued over trivial things. One morning, we were in those argumentive moods when Brayen lost his temper and slapped me on my bottom. He had never hit me before, but I guess I had it coming. I knew I was not blameless, so when he hit me, I found myself saying to him he should hit me harder. He continued to hit me harder, and I screamed. Then, suddenly, there was a knock on the door. Brayen went to answer it and Tex, the bass player, walked in. I started to complain to him about the ill treatment I was getting from my husband.

Brayen just kept quiet and kept his cool. Maybe he was frightened that Tex might interfere because the latter looked very strong with broad shoulders.

However, while I was still complaining to Tex, Brayen went out of the house.

Tex had the nerve to advise me to call the police and complain that I had been bashed about by my husband. I really do not know why I took his advice and telephoned the police. They asked me if he inflicted any physical injuries to my body. I told them that he hadn't, whereupon they replied by saying that as it was a domestic issue they could not interfere. Had I sustained any injuries, they might have been able to do something about it. So, the matter ended there.

Whilst my relationship with Tex flourished and grew from strength to strength, my husband and I found ourselves progressively estranged from each other as the days rolled by.

Then, into my life was ushered a series of bizarre incidents which hitherto had never been part of my life. I cannot comprehend what emotional, psychological, or other factors made me do the things I found myself doing.

It was a phase of my life which I would rather forget. However, life being what it is, a catalogue of joys, sadness, inhumanities, good, evil, and a host of other experiences, it would be dishonest and foolhardy of me to suppress these events, or to put them in metaphorically to conceal the hideous skeletons in my cupboard.

The series of bizarre incidents started when I used to go window shopping in Portobello Market. I remember on one such adventure, I went into a shop where the sales assistant, a girl of about nineteen years, attended to me. I went into the changing room with three pairs of trousers. When I came out I paid for a pair of corduroy trousers while I concealed two pairs of trousers in my handbag. The state of my mind then must have been one devoid of any moral or ethical sensors.

When I came out of the shop, I do not recall feeling a sense of guilt at that time. But thinking about it now, it was a very horrible thing to have done. Maybe one of the reasons why I did those things was out of necessity; my husband and I were most of the time financially embarrassed. My husband did not buy me clothes often; I had to do some hostesses jobs to make ends meet.

I once went to Oxford Street, whilst in a shop, I felt an irrepressible urge to take something. I took a few clothes into the changing room where I tried them on. As I put a pair of trousers in my bag, a customer opened the curtains and saw me in the process. I thought to myself she was only a customer and there was nothing she could do about it. When I came out of the changing room I saw her in the company of a man whom I suspected was her husband. They talked to a sales assistant upon seeing me; the lady who had seen me in the changing room pointed at me. Defensively, I retraced my steps and found myself running and meandering through several racks of clothes. When I looked behind me, I saw the man whom I suspected was the customer's husband coming at me. I quickly leapt into an escalator going down to the ground floor. When I got there, I dashed to the other escalator going upstairs. In the meantime, my mind was busy trying to work out a way of getting me out of the jam I was in. When I got upstairs, I decided to go back to the changing room where I removed the pair of trousers from my bag and left it in the room.

I stayed there for a few minutes to calm myself down before I went out. The man who had given me a chase had returned to the woman who had reported me to the sales assistant. I decided to make a purchase. I took a dress to the cash register and was about to pay for it, when suddenly, I became aware of the presence of the female assistant I had been reported to. With her was a man I believe was the manager.

She challenged me and said she believed I had something concealed in my handbag. I replied that there was nothing in my bag. I was searched. They apologized to me when they found nothing, but the man who had chased me remarked that I had dropped whatever I took in the changing room. I left the shop relieved, probably not knowing how lucky I was not to get caught red-handed.

This phase of my life coincided with my attempts to form a band. With the assistance of Tex, I got a few musicians who I invited to stay at my house. It proved to be an enormous responsibility, because, although they lived there on an on-and-off basis, they didn't contribute financially toward food. I also had to foot the expenses for running the basement we used for rehearsals.

With these commitments weighing heavily on my almost non-existent resources, I found myself going to a supermarket in Notting Hill Gate to steal food to feed the musicians. My husband was well aware of the goings on, but in his usual manner, he did not approve or disapprove.

Some of the items of food I stole included things like chicken, ham, and coffee. I did this on about four occasions. Each time I came back home with so called "loot," the musicians always cheered and congratulated me. They made me feel like a heroine.

But like everything else in this world, nothing lasts forever. I went into the same supermarket one day and put some items of food into my bag. As I was coming out of the supermarket, a woman dressed in ordinary clothes grabbed my hand very hard. "Excuse me, I want to search you," she said in a very stern voice. I knew she was a store detective. I had the fright of my life. I struggled to get out of her grip. As I was struggling, a crowd suddenly grew around us. The customers who were coming out of the supermarket and also the passers-by stopped to find out what was going on. My heart pounded in fear. In desperation, I started to scream. I thought I had nothing to lose screaming, so I continued to scream at the top of my voice. Some people in the crowd asked her to leave me alone as she tried to explain to them that I had stolen something.

Then, the manager of the supermarket came out wearing white overalls. She told the store detective to let me go, who was very reluctant. As soon as she released her grip from my hand, I left the items I had taken on the floor, took my bag, and hurried away. Looking back, I think if the manager hadn't let me go, possibly, it would have been bad publicity for the supermarket if they had insisted in creating a drama over the issue.

However, I started running as fast as I could. I remember seeing a policeman and thinking to myself that if he had been on the scene about two minutes earlier, he should have taken me away. I ran to the underground station through the subway.

It was such a profound experience, that, after that, I swore it would never happen again in my life. Never again did I attempt to pinch anything that didn't belong to me. The fright evoked by that experience was such an overpowering deterrent that I never attempted to do it again.

CHAPTER NINE

I

During the first two years of my stay in Notting Hill Gate, I had a pretty good relationship with Mary, the English lady who occupied the ground floor and the basement. But that cordial relationship soon came to an end when she moved out of the flat because she had found a better flat somewhere else.

Her stepsister, a very pretty woman, and her husband, a man of quiet disposition, moved into the flat. They were a Jewish couple who liked to play down the fact that they were Jews. They had no children of their own but adopted two children, a boy and a girl. The couple wrote children's books.

We were not the best neighbors. Most of the reasons why we exchanged angry words were because my son, Jerom, who was just over three years then, used to run across the floor. She would telephone me from downstairs to tell me to control him. I found it ridiculous because I believed my son had the right to play around in the afternoon, and it was almost impossible to control or curtail the playing habits of a child of Jerom's age. In addition to ringing me about four times a week, she wrote a letter to the company that let the house, saying that my son was a nuisance.

One day, with the intention of having a bath, I ran the water in the bath while I kept my husband and some friends company in the living room. I guess we must have been so engrossed with the conversation we were having, that it escaped my memory that I had left the tap running.

Our conversation was interrupted by a vicious knock on the door. The suddenness of the knock made us a bit apprehensive. Then there followed a barrage of banging on the door. When we opened it, the couple downstairs stood outside fuming and livid with anger, and I guess, justifiably too. They said there was water leaking through into their flat from the ceiling, and they had good reason to believe it came from our floor.

Remembering I had left the tap running, I rushed to the bathroom and turned off the tap. The bath was full, and there was a pool of water on the floor.

My husband and I were very apologetic about what happened, but our previous relationship did not help matters. They asked us to come down and see the damage we had done. My husband and I followed them down the hallway where we saw a large hole in the ceiling from which water was dripping. The ceiling was not in the best conditions, and I suspected that the previous occupants of the flat must have encountered similar problems of water leaking from the ceiling, as it didn't look as if it was newly created.

There was a bookshelf in the middle of the floor which had been soiled. The whole flat was in a state for disarray; it was as if a cyclone had hit the place.

Still apologizing, my husband and I offered to help clean up and repair the ceiling at our own expense. They refused. When we had gone upstairs, they came up to us again, complaining how irresponsible they thought we were. Again, we offered to clean up the mess, but they refused bluntly. We had no choice but to continue to beg them. Our pleas fell on deaf ears. They insisted that they wanted someone from the company who let the place to see the damage we had done to their property.

It transpired that they wrote a letter to the company relating to them what had happened and giving them an evaluation of what they thought was the damage done to their property. The company, in turn, sent us a strongly worded letter in which they included the fact that we would have to pay for the cost of the repairs. It took about six months before the builders came over to fix the damage. We paid about fifty pounds for the repair.

In the meantime, the couple continued their hostility toward us, trying, psychologically, everything they had in their armory to get us out of the flat. The company too had an axe to grind with us and would have been very pleased to see us out of the premises. When we first moved in, our rent was fifteen pounds a week, which at that time was an exorbitant amount to pay. Some friends advised us to take the matter up with the Rent Tribunal, which we did. The Rent Tribunal decided that our rent was going to be reduced to nine pounds.

In the midst of the cat and dog relationship we had with the Jewish couple downstairs, the frictions in my relationship with my husband widened, while Tex and I grew to like each other more and more.

One day, Brayen told me he wanted to go to France to visit Mario, his Italian friend who had attended our wedding. He reckoned he would be there for about three of four weeks. When he left, I began to see more of Tex. We used to go to the rehearsal room together where we jammed with the other musicians.

I thought it would be a good idea if I could rent the rehearsal room to other musicians and make some money in the meantime, in addition to using it for my own purposes. So, I advertised in the *Melody Maker* about letting the place out for rehearsals. Somehow, the owner of the place, a Greek man, who also owned a fish and chip shop, got wind of the fact that I was going to let the place out, so he demanded I pay him more for the rent of the place. I told him the rehearsal room was not worth the extra money he was demanding because it was very damp and filthy. As a matter of fact, most of the musicians who paid to rehearse in the place were so disgusted with the filth that they disappeared without bothering to ask for their money back.

In the end, the landlord and I came to compromise on the figure of seven pounds a week, because I couldn't let it out to other musicians.

My husband came back from France after about three weeks stay there. About two days after he returned, he lost his temper while we were having breakfast. It was over some trivial thing. It was very unusual for him to overreact the way he did. He took a glass of milk which he smashed on the table. Jerom, who was sitting very close to him, fell out of his chair while we were arguing. When I looked at him on the floor, I noticed he was bleeding.

As I told Brayen to look at what he had done to my son, he left the house without trying to find out if the injury was serious or not. There was a cut running across his upper lip toward his nose. I started panicking because I didn't quite know what to do.

I went downstairs to the Jewish couple and told them that my son had sustained an injury and needed help. The fact that we were not on good terms didn't enter my mind. They came upstairs very reluctantly and the man offered to take us to the hospital in his car. He was very cold about it. It was evident in his manner that he did it in spite of himself.

When we arrived at the hospital, they examined Jerom, and the doctor informed me that he had to remove some particles of glass that were in his eye. I was very worried as to whether his vision would be impaired in any way. Luckily, the particles of glass were removed successfully, and his vision was not affected. He had about four stitches above his upper lip.

The deteriorating relationship between my husband and I was not helped by the fact that he walked out on me and my son, who was bleeding. I saw it as an act of wickedness and hated him for it.

After that incident, I ceased to have any modicum of respect for my husband. We had both crossed the rubicund of love. I invited Tex to come and live with us. He hesitated, initially, but not for long. He moved in after a few days. We had a very strange arrangement in the house.

My husband and Jerom slept in the big bedroom while Tex and I slept in the small room. Funnily enough, there seemed to be no ill feeling over the arrangement. My husband went to work as usual and appeared unconcerned and detached from all the happenings. But beneath that air of unconcern and feeling of detachment, he was working out something. The crunch came when one day I saw him packing all his belongings.

I asked him what he was doing. He replied that he was moving out of the house. I was quite taken aback. I didn't want him to leave. Naively, I asked him why he wanted to leave. He said he just wanted to leave. I guess he thought every human being has an elastic limit, and he had been stretched to that limit.

Maybe, maybe not. He was a strange man who never had a straight talk with me. There was no meeting of minds between us. He never offered me advice on any issue or told me off when I did something indecent. I never knew how he felt about the bad things or wrong things that I was doing; he just never really tried to educate me or talk to me about it. In my state of mind, I was still wild.

Even before he left the house unceremoniously, he did not bother to bring me back to earth by saying something about the folly or wisdom of the affair I had been having with the bass player, Tex. He left the way I had met him.

II

If I were superstitious, I would have believed that my husband's undignified exit from our matrimonial home was a bad omen for me, a sign that there was something disastrous in the offering, and he didn't want to hang around to pick up the pieces when that disaster struck.

But I'm not superstitious, at least not with such things. Although I did not want him to leave, the actual departure was a nonevent for me. I did not lose any sleep over it, I didn't pull my hair out either.

The first two days after my husband departed saw the apogee of my relationship with Tex. Everything seemed to work like clockwork. It seemed we would be free and happy thereafter, but after these two days, the solid foundation flawed. Probably, Tex subconsciously saw himself playing a new role as master of the house, to whom I should play a second fiddle. On the other hand, he probably did what he did because his drug-abused mind no longer distinguished between propriety and impropriety.

I remember I was preparing some meatballs for dinner with a few musicians, and I had left the kitchen temporarily with the meatballs in a Pyrex bowl. Suddenly, I saw the keyboard player gesticulating to me quietly to come into the kitchen. When I went into the kitchen, he showed me what had happened to the meatballs. Tex had poured washing up liquid on them for no apparent reason. Although the keyboard player tried to rinse the meatballs and hamburgers, I had to throw them away because they were not fit for consumption. Tex offered some apologies for doing what he had done, but it was difficult to take the apology seriously because it was the act of a man out of his mind.

A couple of days after that, I was lying in bed with him, when suddenly, he slapped me on the face with all his strength. The slap was so hard that my face became red and left an imprint of his finger marks upon my face. I was scared out of my wits because I had not provoked him. The thought occurred to me that he could be going crazy.

I rushed, screaming, to a female acquaintance of mine who was staying with me at that time. I was so frightened by the whole incident that I left the flat. I was shedding tears as I walked toward Portobello Market. At the market, I saw an acquaintance who asked me what the matter was.

I told him that my husband had walked out of the home and a boyfriend had been staying with me. I told him I did not really know what this boyfriend was capable of doing or not doing; that it seemed I had misjudged his character because he had slapped me very hard on the face without being provoked at all. The acquaintance advised me that the best course of action would be to go to the police and report the incident.

I went to the police and told them everything that had happened. After listening to my story, they said there was nothing they could do about it.

The thought of going back to the flat with him still around sent shivers down my spine. I had to get rid of him because I now considered him a threat to me. Since he had hit me once, he may hit me again. That was a risk I was not prepared to take.

While I was pondering on what to do, the idea suddenly occurred to me that a sure way of getting rid of him was to tell the police he was involved in drugs. So, I told them he had a lot of drugs and hashish in his possession. On hearing that, the police became very interested. I also told them where to find the stuff in a special drawer where he kept them. The police told me they were going to pay him a surprise visit, and they wanted me to be away from the flat for a while.

When I left the police station, I just wandered around trying to kill time. I went back to the flat a few hours later to find he was not there, but he came back later that day in a very melancholy mood.

He told me, with eyes full of tears, that the police had advised him to get out of the flat, but he told me he wanted to stay. I told him he couldn't stay because I had had enough of his violence. He started crying and hitting the wall with both hands like a spoilt child. While he was doing this, I became slightly worried that he may refuse to leave. If he did that, there was nothing I could really do about it. But fortunately for me, when he found I was not giving ground to his appeals, he decided to pack his things and leave.

He was charged in court. I felt sorry for him, and I was going to tell the court that he was not really a pusher, and that some friends had actually brought the stuff there. That, I thought, would mitigate the gravity of the jam I had thrown him into.

However, when the case was called in court, it was dismissed because it was discovered that the stuff he had was not hashish, but henna, a weed used for hair treatment.

He got the stuff from our drummer who we used to watch prepare it in his flat. He usually boiled the stuff and added water to it intermittently. He told us that was how hashish was made. At times, he sold us some of it, but occasionally, we smoked it without paying for it. Each time we smoked it, we used to have headaches. At that time, we thought it was because it was low-quality hashish; we didn't realize it was henna.

Soon after that incident, I received a letter from my sister, Debra, who was in Israel at that time. Her two children were with her husband in Canada. In her letter, she said she was going to come to London. She also expressed the fear that because of an affair she had with a man in Israel, she thought her husband would not want to take her back as a wife. She later joined me in London.

After the departure of my husband, Brayen, I managed to contact Dadley, the blonde Englishman that was instrumental in my meeting Brayen.

Dadley was the legitimate father of my son. His coming to my place was anticlimatic. There was nothing friendly or warm about him. He came like a stranger, not as an old friend. Debra was around when he came.

I told her he used to be my boyfriend, but I was no longer going out with him. I cannot explain why I did it, but I found myself trying to impress on her how very handsome Dadley was.

Later, she asked me if it would be alright if they both went out together. I had no objections. They went to a pub. When they returned, they locked themselves in the small room.

I wanted to find out what was going on, so I peeped through the key hole and saw my sister naked. Dadley was playing with her. I was annoyed, maybe I was jealous.

The next day, they went on out again and came back very late. They knocked on the door, but I ignored them. After knocking a few more times, Dadley smashed the glass part of the door.

I was furious when I discovered what had happened. I started threatening to call the police. I guess that must have frightened Dadley because he left the house immediately, while Debra went after him.

After about an hour, she came back alone. She said she could not keep pace with his quick, long strides; he had left her running behind him. After calling his name a few times without hearing an answer, she decided to come back home. That was the last we saw of Dadley.

No sooner was that incident with Dadley over, than my manager came over to my place and became interested in Debra. I told my sister who he was and that his family was well to do. He took her out and bought her an overcoat because it was winter and she hadn't brought any coat from Israel. Debra did not like him and wanted to avoid him as much as possible.

One day, he came over with the intention of taking her out. I told her he was around and that she should hide in the bathroom. When he asked me where she was, I told him she was out. He must have sensed I was telling him lies, because after he left the flat, he telephoned me later to say he knew Debra was in when he came. He accused me of not wanting him to go out with my sister.

That seemed to be the final nail in the coffin of my business relationship with him. He became disenchanted and fed up with me. Because he wasn't doing anything for me, I got in touch with Equity with a view to releasing myself contractually from him. I gave a lawyer attached to Equity all the necessary details. Within a few weeks, I received a letter of release. It didn't cost me anything. Maybe it was due to the fact that I was a member of Equity.

Because my husband did not send me any money, and I had no source of income, I decided to start living off welfare. With my poor financial position, I could not offer my sister, Debra, anything. I tried to effect reconciliation between her and her husband for her children's sake and the fact that I did not see her making a good future out of her life by remaining in England. I wrote letters and telegrams to her husband in Canada convincing him that she had turned a new leaf and wanted to join him. Whenever he telephoned me, he always refused to talk to her. After considerable pressure from me, he finally gave in and sent her a plane ticket to go back to Canada.

Debra discovered when she was sent back to Canada that while she was away, her husband had brought another woman into the house, and that was why, initially, he did not want her back. This woman had stolen most of Debra's clothes when she finally left the house.

After Debra's departure, I became very lonely with my son, Jerom. Life became very boring for me. I wanted to have Brayen back. I used to call him at work, telling him to come and pay me a visit.

When he came around one day, I told him I was going to sell the record player because I was financially embarrassed. The next morning, I saw him removing the stereo set. As he was walking down the staircase with it, I gave him a push in the back. He almost fell down. That was the first time I had done anything like that. I was not, by nature, a person given to violence.

I continued to call my husband at work telling him to come back. I guess he got fed up with the calls. He told his supervisor that whenever I telephoned, he should tell me never to call again.

I became very sad and depressed because I wasn't happy. I saw my family doctor and told him about my problems. He recommended that I see a psychiatrist. The psychiatrist suggested if the pressure was too much for me to bear, he could admit me to a mental hospital for awhile for treatment. I didn't want to be separated from my son, so I decided I would rather see the psychiatrist once every two weeks, rather than be admitted into a hospital.

Just over the road from my house lived a star called Twiggy, who lived with her manager. I used to watch her admiringly as she walked to her chauffeur-driven Bentley. I was always thinking to myself, that with my talent as a singer, if I approached them, they may be able to give me some kind of assistance.

One day, I summoned up some courage and knocked on their door. Her manager opened the door for me. I told him I was a singer and that I had in my possession some demos I had recorded with some musicians, and I wondered if he could help me.

He invited me in. Twiggy looked like a beautiful princess, sitting watching a color television in an exquisitely furnished living room. He took me upstairs to his office. Twiggy was so engrossed watching the television that she didn't even turn around to see who it was that had come in.

While we were upstairs, I showed him the demos, and he told me he had a friend who worked in Apple Records, which belonged to the Beatles. He added that he would give the demos to his friend and that I should come back in a few weeks to find out if they liked them or not.

I was very elated when I left his office that day because I thought something good may come out of my meeting him.

After a few weeks, I went back to him. I told him some biographical information about myself. I asked him if he was a Jew because he looked like one. He said no, but he had a wife who was Jewish and that accounted for why he could not marry Twiggy. He told me how he was principally responsible in making her a star by sending her photographs to many fashion houses but not allowing them to always use her. By making her very scarce, she became sought after and in very great demand.

As we continued in this conversational mood, he tried to put his hands over me when the long, black wig I had on fell off from my head. He appeared to be shocked by that incident, which I believe must have put him off. He immediately recoiled away from me and suddenly looked the respectable businessman he would like me to think he was. He said his friend who worked in Apple Records hadn't sent back the demos and that I should come back in another few weeks. I could detect a note of dismissal in his tone, so I decided it was time for me to leave.

I went back after a few weeks and he handed me the demos, saying curtly, that they were not interested in them.

III

I was trying to escape from loneliness. As a child, I was a very lonely person. As an adult, though there were often too many things happening to me and around me, I did not have the time to brood, analyze my life, or my future. I was just moving, doing, and being a robot.

At twenty-six, all I had was my son. He meant everything to me. He was, and remains, the jewel of my heart. Besides that, I had little to show for my life in terms of success. My career as a singer, apart from a brief spell with my music teacher, Nahoun Nardi, of blessed memory, never really got off the ground.

I always seemed not to be in the right place at the right time. Most people seem to have breaks, but that is something I was starved of. I see, around me, people with less talent making it to the top. I'm neither jealous nor envious of them. I just bide my time and live in the hope that my time will come. I don't kid myself that it will be easy. I lack the discipline that is indispensable in making me comport myself. I must be disciplined and forward-looking.

Ambition is something I possess, what I do lack is the wherewithal to transform those ambitions in order to begin my realities. Because of the weakness of my defense mechanisms to cope effectively with the turmoil that often plagues me, I found myself sinking from one level of depression to another.

A few weeks after my hopes of something fruitful coming out of the submission of my demos to Apple Records were dashed to the wall, my emotional state deteriorated from bad to worse. I would cry all night wondering if my vicissitudes could ever be reversed. I wrote several letters to Debra in Canada telling her of my feelings and state of mind.

She telephoned me one night suggesting I go over to Canada to pick up the threads and start anew. It was music to my ears, and it sounded like the kind of break I needed.

The next day, I sold all the items of furniture in the house, the proceeds to be used to purchase my flight ticket to Canada. By the second week, I was set to go to what I thought was a land of opportunity where my potential as a singer would achieve the status of actuality.

With my son Jerom, I flew to Canada to join Debra. Inviting me to join her in Canada was a fantastic gesture to the credit of my sister. At the time it was made, I suppose it was done with the best of intentions. But the whole atmosphere when I got there reeked of superficiality and artificiality. Everything seemed plastic to me. I was not happy. Right from the beginning, I realized my grand plans about making it in Canada were a pipedream, an illusion.

Debra had a small carpet business and often left to work in the shop in the mornings, while I stayed at home and took care of her children. I felt ill at ease because she didn't leave any instructions or discuss anything about cooking or eating. All the food stuff was frozen in the freezer.

I once saw her giving her children fresh slices of bread while she was giving my son dry bread. I hated the preferential treatment she meted out on the children.

In spite of the fact that I was living with her, I still had my sense of justice and pride. Her children also had petty squabbles with Jerom. They complained about him playing with their toys and things. They gave the impression he was depriving them of their possessions.

A few days after I arrived, I accompanied my sister and her husband to a club where a band was entertaining. As the evening wore on, Debra began to show signs of developing a liking for a member of the band. Though I was not directly involved, it was an awkward situation for me. She wanted to leave with this member of the band. I had to bring her back to earth and point out to her what the implications of what she was trying to do would be.

In the end, she saw reason and stayed with us. While this was going on, her husband was swearing. He lacked effective control over her. Like always, whenever her passions led her astray, he was ever ready to take her back.

About two days after that episode, I saw them take masculine pills and lie on the bed. They were there for awhile, when, suddenly, I heard Debra call me. She wanted me to join them in bed. I took it to be an innocuous invitation, and I didn't want to be antisocial or a killjoy. I joined them.

I watched them play with each other. Debra wanted me to join them. I was not used to orgies, so I declined. I just lie down on the bed as if paralyzed.

In response to my nonchalant attitude, in an outburst of rage, she accused me of not loving her as a sister. She said if I did love her, I should at least have kissed her. I was disgusted by the whole incident.

Later, I told her husband that I couldn't take part in the orgy because I was not used to it. I added that it would be a different thing if it were sex involving only him and me. I am not quite sure if, at that time, I meant it or not. Her husband later told her that I was trying to take him to bed. This provoked another row between my sister an I. She accused me of attempting to take her husband to bed and of hating her because I convinced her husband to take her back while she was staying with me in London. To her, I did that because I didn't want her to be around. In the course of exchanging angry words, she said my behavior frightened her. Considering the weird incidents that happened since I arrived, I told her if there was anybody that had the potential to frighten anyone, it was her.

Because of these unfortunate developments, I told her I was going to leave. She didn't try to stop me. I decided I was going to America, to an aunt of mine who lived in New York.

Her husband was kind enough to me and gave me $100 to pay for my flight. I booked a flight to Montréal where I hoped to go to the American Embassy there for a visa. Things didn't work the way I had planned. When I got to the embassy, much to my bewilderment, I was refused a visa. The visa officer claimed I should have applied for one in London. I found myself in a very tight spot. I didn't know anybody in Montréal, I had no money to check into a hotel, and there was no flight to London I could take that day. I had just enough money for my flight back to London. So, I decided I was going to spend the night in the airport with my son and possibly sleep on a bench.

While I was in the airport, I confided in one of the female assistants who worked for one of the airlines, telling her of my predicament. Before I knew what was happening, she had arranged, with her colleagues, a cash contribution made for me. That night, they checked me into a very good hotel where I had a very superb dinner. It was an experience I would never forget. I couldn't express my gratitude in words.

The next day, I caught a plane to London, where, waiting for me, was the somber reality that I had no home. Although I still had my piano in my former flat, I had forfeited my tenancy. Some people advised me to break into the flat, but I thought otherwise.

Because of the bad patch I was going through, I got in touch with my mother-in-law and asked if she could care for Jerom until I was fully capable of fending for and taking good care of him. I thought it was not fair for him to go through those hard times with me. It was in 1971, and he was only five and a half years old.

My mother-in-law agreed to take care of him. I managed to stay with some friends while I tried to sort things out for myself. Things were not easy. I had no job and therefore no sources of income. When I had outstayed my time with friends, I secured a room in the worst part of Portobello Market.

I used to search through the newspapers looking for job advertisements. One day, I saw an advert for a hostess in a West End club. I applied for the job and got it. It involved sitting and drinking with male clients, making them spend money in the club by buying drinks. I was paid on commission from how much they spent.

It was common practice for some of the hostesses to go home with the clients. I did that a few times. Really, I was like a fish out of water. I was not suited for that kind of life. I got the sack from the proprietors of the club because they thought I was not good enough. They felt I was not pushing the clients hard enough to part with their money.

Thus, I was back to square one, back to the drawing room, in a manner of speaking.

CHAPTER TEN

I

Try as I could, my attempts to get myself settled were unsuccessful. In my desperation, I tried to contact anybody I had known in my past.

I managed to get in touch with Gavel, the fiery Englishman, who, with his wife, had accompanied Dadley to visit me in Paris in response to my request that I wanted to see Dadley about my pregnancy.

Gavel ran a private school in Chalk Farm. He lived in a very large house which had three big bedrooms upstairs and a few rooms downstairs. Also living in the house was a lecturer from the private school. The lecturer was also English, a product of Cambridge University, who was heavily involved in drugs.

Having seen the place, I decided I was going to move in and Gavel had no objections. Although, when he paid me a visit, I witnessed the sado-masochistic relationship he had with his wife who had since left him, I didn't think of the consequences of what living with him would entail. Reflections were a luxury I could not afford. My main pre-occupation was getting myself a house, a place to sleep at night.

Gavel was a man who prided himself in his intellect, always philosophizing in very flamboyant language. He had a very sharp tongue which could be likened to a lethal weapon.

Living in his house was quite an experience. It was a very busy place flowing with people. It was also very filthy. I kept myself busy cleaning the filth and trying to restore some sanity to the place.

Late one night, we were both tripping (to use the language of drug users). He started to attack me verbally with his usual grandiloquence. We were never on the same wavelength. His language was that of erudition, mine was the language of the street. On this particular night, his verbosity was directed at my personality, how intolerant he thought I was. I think he had a complex about his sexuality. He was impotent. I think his verbal aggressiveness was an attempt to make up for what he thought he lacked in sexual prowess.

I threatened him, as he bombarded me with words, that if he persisted, I was going to slash my wrists. I think, subconsciously, I also wanted to know how much he cared for me. If he cared, he would not allow me to slash my wrists. When I could no longer stand the pressure of his attacks, I decided to leave him and go upstairs. As I ascended the staircase, he followed me, his attack unrelenting. Just outside the bathroom upstairs was a wooden shelf where he kept his shaving kit. As I passed by, I saw a razor blade which

I picked up. Oblivious of the full impact of what I was trying to do, I slashed my wrist with the blade. For the first few seconds, it seemed no serious damage had been done. A thin horizontal cut appeared across the wrist, then after about twenty seconds, there were spurts of blood which gushed out intermittently.

Suddenly, the blood started flowing like a tap. I became panic stricken. The sight of the blood did not move Gavel. He persisted in his verbal attacks.

I reached for a big towel and put it across the cut, trying to stop the bleeding. The towel was covered in blood within the twinkling of an eye. I rushed to the room where the lecturer stayed and knocked frantically on the door. I must have woken him up from a very deep sleep. I showed him my bleeding wrist and asked him to telephone for an ambulance. The sight of blood did not make much impact on him. His reactions were sluggish; they were not that of a man reacting to an emergency. Taking his time, he went downstairs and telephoned for an ambulance.

The ambulance took me to the emergency ward at about two o'clock in the morning. I had eight stitches in the left wrist. I was told I didn't know how lucky I was. If the cut had been deeper, my left hand would have been amputated. I came back from the hospital the next day. The news of my attempted suicide spread like a prairie fire within, and beyond, the vicinity of Chalk Farm. It was hardly surprising, when, a few days later, the rector of the private school, who had been away in the country with one of the lectures, took a very dim view of what had happened. He ordered that I leave the premises because the lecturers and the school had a reputation to maintain.

I tried to persuade him to temper justice with mercy by allowing me to remain but to no avail.

Gavel's "I don't care" attitude continued. To him, what had happened to me was inconsequential. Later, I heard that the next girlfriend he had after me stabbed him with a knife, and he even lacked the guts to report the matter to the police.

However, following my ejection from the premises, a young English fellow, who was about twenty-five, who used to come around the house, offered me his room which was situated about two streets away. The offer was standing until I was able to secure a place of my own. In the meantime, he said he would be living with his parents.

I think he liked me; that was why he made me the offer. He made me go to bed with him, presumably, as payment for the favor he had rendered me. Although I appreciated his offer, I did not like him as a person to have to go to bed with, but in view of my position, I suppose I really had no choice but to give in. I guess it helped to get the feeling of indebtedness I felt off my chest. Come to think of it, in the circumstances, if I was to forge ahead, I had to make sacrifices like that. Because my stay there was temporary, I tried to secure a job so that when I got a place of my own, I would be able to afford the rent and deposit.

My choice of jobs was very limited. I had no real vocation for which I was qualified. I had no steady life. I had no opportunity to further my meager education.

My English was not so good. The only language I understood and spoke fluently was Hebrew, which would not get me anywhere in England.

The only job that I had a chance of getting, apart from singing, was as a hostess, The job needed no special qualifications except for the fact that one had to be pretty and attractive to men. I possessed these two qualities. After job hunting for a few days, I found a job in a club in Covent Garden.

The club was run by a young Englishman who seemed to be obsessed with reggae music. One evening, he invited me and one other hostess, a black girl, to where he stayed outside London. We went in his car, a gleaming Rolls Royce, which was well-equipped with a portable color television, cassette recorder, and the whole works. Throughout the journey reggae music blasted from the powerful loudspeakers.

The place was a villa, which, at first sight, looked like a millionaire's hide out. It was a massive place, fully equipped with things that reeked of extravagance.

As we entered the villa, facing us was an indoor swimming pool. Sitting by the swimming pool were four youngsters who must have been in their late teens. Beside them were two middle-aged men dressed in expensive suits, who, I later gathered, were well to do lawyers who owned the club my boss ran. They were all smoking pot and drinking alcohol.

We did not get friendly reception from them for reasons which later became obvious to me. My boss told us that the young men were members of a pop group, and they were being nurtured and helped by the two lawyers in getting recording contracts and the like. For the services the lawyers rendered to them, they had homosexual relationships with them. It was hardly surprising when our arrival looked almost an intrusion into their exclusive preserve and privacy. My boss left me by the swimming pool while he took the black girl away upstairs. I sat there feeling very bored, when, suddenly, one of the boys came over to me with a towel around his waist. As he stood in front of me, he opened his towel and exposed his private parts to me. I was a bit shocked by this piece of exhibitionism. After about an hour, the black girl came downstairs for me.

I followed her into a bedroom, where, lying on the bed was my boss. The black girl joined him in bed while he told me to remove my clothes and join them. I joined them in bed but only in a passive capacity. The black girl seemed to like him quite a lot. She stuck to him like a tick. They made love to each other most of the night. I didn't participate because orgies did nothing for me. My boss was a very attractive man, but he was not really my type; I didn't like him.

The next morning, I walked around the villa out of curiosity. I saw a grand piano in a very large room which was probably provided for the members of the group to practice on. Though a lot of money had been spent on the place, it did not look like the kind of place a family lived in. It was filthy. It lived up to what it looked like: a place for orgies and homosexual affairs.

Later that morning, my boss drove us back to London. On our way, I complimented him by saying he lived very well. He acknowledged the compliment and added that the two lawyers are jealous because he went around with women; because they were homosexuals, they also fancied him.

II

A few minutes' walk from the new club I was working in, lived a middle-aged Englishman who was one of the club's regular customers. He was not endowed with very attractive features; in fact, he was a grotesque looking specimen of manhood. But what he lacked in good looks, he more than made up in material possessions.

He was a very wealthy man whose financial interests include a service station, numerous caravans, and a successful launderette, not to mention landed property. He struck a quick friendship with me when he saw me in the club during one of his frequent visits. At the early stage of my acquaintance with him, I mentioned to him during the course of a conversation that I was looking for a place to rent. He said in his house he normally had about two or three rooms which he rented out, but they were not available at that time. However, he said until one of them became vacant, I could live with him. I accepted the invitation and moved in.

The next day, he took me to a restaurant. That was the beginning of about six embarrassing outings to restaurants I had with him. During these outings, he always displayed his uncouthness and bad manners. He drank himself drunk and shouted at the waiters who politely asked him to pay the bill and leave. Going out with him was a terrible ordeal because what would happen was always a foregone conclusion.

Certain evenings, I gave him a hand in counting silver coins he had in sacks, which were proceeds from the washing machines and tumble dryers he had in the launderette, which was below the flat he lived in. There were times he felt in a generous mood and gave me some money. He used to suggest that I give up working in the club as a hostess. I always replied to him that I would like to, but I could not at that time because I had no source of income, coupled with the fact that, because I had very little vocational training, my chances of getting another job were very slim.

About five days after I started living with him, he took me to Surrey one weekend to spend some time in the beautiful country house he owned up on a hill. Like him, his mother was very wealthy too. She was a woman who made a great impression on people. Hearing her speak, one knew instinctively that she was a very good businesswoman, hard, shrewd, and intelligent.

We came back to London after the weekend of living in his country house of purple of luxury. However, in spite of his affluence, I did not really get on with him, primarily because of his drunken stupors and the fact that as soon as he was drunk, he became intolerable.

I lived with him for two weeks, until, one day, he told me, that one of the rooms he let upstairs was vacant, and that if I wanted it, he could let it out to me. The manner in which he said it made me presume he was terminating our short-lived relationship.

The rooms he let upstairs were scarcely furnished; the one that I had, had no cooking facilities. There was only a bed, a few items of furniture, and a sink to wash the face in.

Not long after I settled in the room, I lost my job in the club because I refused to be submissive to the young, male members of the management who expected me to be at their disposal. They conspired to have me terminated. I looked for another club to work in for a few days, until I found one in Soho, which was not too far away from where I lived in Covent Garden. It was a small but decent basement club. My stay there was very brief; I got the sack after just four days because, in the opinion of the management, I was not treating the clients nicely. It was expected from me to let them take full liberties with me.

At this stage, becoming fired frequently was now an accepted occupational hazard for me; an unpleasant fact I had to live with.

I managed to find another club in Soho which was just a room in a house. The club was filthy and dark; the walls were in a state of disrepair and the furniture antiquated.

In fact, it was more like a prostitute's haven than a nightclub. Not surprisingly, I could not bear to stay in the club for two days. I left on my own volition.

I began to think seriously of saving as much money as I could to go back to Israel to start a new life. I could not resign myself to perpetually living the life of a hostess or a prostitute. Necessity and the urge to survive were alienating me from my true self. I was in bondage and being enslaved. My passions were not suited for that kind of existence.

The West End of London, especially Soho, had very bad memories for me. They provided the scenario and setting for a period of my life where I stumbled from one filthy club to another, all in the name of eking out subsistence. However, there are times when out of the bad may come forth good.

The turning point came when I managed to find another club to work in. It was also in Soho, and it was the last club I had to work in. It was a small club whose atmosphere and modest surroundings were more respectable than most of the previous clubs I had worked in.

One evening, three respectably dressed men walked into the club. They seated themselves down and started conversing in French. They looked like business men to me. I went up to one of them, who appeared to have friendly air about him, and asked him if he would cherish my company. He was full of smiles as he replied in the affirmative. He was about fifty-five years old. He introduced himself as Robert from a French-speaking area in Switzerland. His friends were also Swiss.

I sat down close to him while his friends were in a deep conversation in French. He bought a bottle of champagne that we shared between us. I literally spent the whole evening with him as we talked about this and that while sipping our drinks.

When they were ready to leave the club, I asked him if I could go with him. He said that I could. I had put his thoughts into words. Together with his friends, we took a taxi to the hotel where they were staying.

When we arrived there, I accompanied him to his room while his friends went to their respective rooms.

I stood very close to the wardrobe in his room while he changed into his pajamas and lay on the bed. I was very suspicious of men in general. I did not trust Robert. I told him before I went to bed with him he must pay me first. We had a slight argument. He said he was going to give me half that night and the remainder the following morning. After a bit of persuasion as to his honest intentions, I joined him in bed.

The cigars he smoked caused the horrible smell of nicotine on his breathe. I could not sleep all night because I was restless and uncomfortable.

In the morning, we had breakfast in his room. Thereafter, we arranged that I would take him around and see a few places of interest.

We spent most of the day in Piccadilly Circus, where I took him into several cafes and shops. He bought me a twenty-pound sapphire ring from a jeweler's shop. During the course of my taking him around, he told me that his presence in London was because he had accompanied the Swiss national football teams who were due to play England in an international match at Wimbley Stadium.

Toward the evening, I took him to where I lived in Covent Garden. While he was there, I narrated to him the circumstances that had led me to live the way I was. Because he seemed very friendly and rich, I asked him if he would do me a favor and help me financially. I told him I needed the money to transport my son, myself, and a few belongings to Israel, where I hoped to start a new life.

He did not make any outright response to my request; instead, he put his hand over my shoulder and insinuated we go to bed together. I was not in the mood for lovemaking, so I politely declined the offer.

However, I gave him my address and told him that in a few weeks' time I hope I would be able to save enough money to pay my fare home. He took the address and promised he was going to pay me a visit in Israel. I did not take what he said seriously.

During the next few days, I used to hang around Park Lane, which was the Mecca for private clubs, high rollers, gamblers, and where such well-known hotels like the Hilton and the Dorchester hotel were situated.

One day, a policeman on patrol followed me and stopped me. He warned me that it was an offence to solicit men.

A couple of weeks later, I managed to save enough money to purchase flight tickets for my son and me. I went to my mother-in-law's house in New Eltham and told her that I wanted my son because I was going back to Israel to start a new life.

I figured that once I got to Israel, I would be able to turn over a new leaf. Although the urge to survive would still be in me, it would not drive me to extremes similar to what happened in London.

I also figured out that I was going to stay with my mother. A few months earlier, word had reached me that my stepfather had died. When he was alive, his attitude toward me was very antagonistic. He never disguised his dislike for me. Had he been still alive, it would have been out of the question to think of staying with my mother.

While I did not rejoice over his death, I had no premonitions or anticipations of any difficulties that may arise out of my living with my mother and her two daughters, who were my stepsisters.

Very early on the day of my departure to Israel, I went to the airport with my luggage, which consisted of three suitcases, an electric piano, and an amplifier. I had not much money left in my possession after purchasing my flight tickets a few days earlier, so I was not in a position to pay for any excess luggage I was likely to incur.

I spoke to one of the officials who worked for the Israeli airline, El-Al, about my difficulty. I told him I left Israel about eight years ago, and I had a rough time and wished to go back to Israel for good, but I had not enough money to pay for any excess luggage.

He was very understanding and sympathetic. He assured me that he would do everything within his power to ensure that I did not pay for any excess luggage. Just as he said, my luggage was carried free of charge.

It is typical for members of my family circle to be very excited and greet with alacrity any member of the family who had been away for a while. The alacrity and hysteria pulls out into nothingness sooner than one realizes it. Members of my family accorded me such a treatment when I arrived in Israel. I stayed in my mother's house as I had planned. My mother's reactions toward me were lukewarm. We had never been close to each other, and I do not think she had ever loved me the way a mother should love a daughter.

I kept a very low profile in everything I did, especially in my social activities. I reckon, subconsciously, I had a complex about going around with men, which was a hangover from my teenage years in Tel-Aviv when people thought I was very promiscuous because of the company of the boyfriends I often kept.

The world of hostessing I was enmeshed in whilst in London, was, for me, the past. It was like a bad dream, and I hoped time would push to the keep recesses of my memory. I was determined and resolute in my conviction not to return to it.

Nevertheless, one thing I could not give up immediately was smoking. I smoked hashish, but very discreetly, at home. I was well aware of the fact that if I smoked it outside or in a public place, the wind of gossip that blew very intensely in Israel, would spread the fact to all and sundry in Tel-Aviv in no time. Memories of the notoriety of my reputation before I left Israel were still rife with me.

One of my stepsisters had a friend called Lenna who lived in a nearby street.

She was about sixteen years old, and every now and then, when she paid us a visit, she used to bring some hashish for me.

I registered Jerom in a nursery school for six-year-olds a few weeks after we arrived in Tel-Aviv.

In the course of time, I came to know a number of famous Israeli musicians, some of whom appeared on television and featured in radio programmes quite often. I was very friendly with one in particular, a saxophonist called Moti Malkom, who had a small brass band that he frequently used for television shows. He became quite close to me. His admiration for me was more than that of a fellow musician appreciating the other. He liked me as a woman and wanted me to have an affair with him although he was a married man. Early in our relationship, I told him that whatever happened between us, he must remain loyal to his wife who had a child from him.

Moti Malkom often told me how good a singer and talented a songwriter he thought I was. Because he was more technically knowledgeable than I was, he helped me rearrange my English and Hebrew songs.

He introduced me to an agent called Pishon who ran an agency called Pashnet in Dissengoff Street in Tel-Aviv. The talent agency was handling most of the famous stars.

Through the agency, I met a well known Israeli singer called Rika Zolee, who wanted to form a trio with two other girls. With one other Israeli girl, who I think came from a Kibbutz, we formed a trio called Guspanka. At the outset, it seemed we were destined for great things. We had three concerts, one television show, and a lot of exposure in the newspapers. However, after that, everything ended in fiasco. I think this was due to two main reasons. The first was that Rika Zolee knew well that the trio threatened to swallow up her fame. Secondly, Moti Malkom, who was the musical director, was trying to make me the lead singer. Thus, the whole arrangement became so disorganized, that inevitably, the trio had to die a natural death.

Unlike my music career, my relationship with Moti Malkom flourished. He used to pay me frequent visits at home, and at times, he took me to hotels. After I had known him for about eight months, I began to be very deeply involved with him emotionally. I missed his company so much that I yearned to see him. I always wanted to be with him. My mother, who knew about the relationship, always told me that he would never leave his wife for me because he was a European Jew, known as the Ashkenazi, and they were prejudice against the Middle Eastern Jews.

151

III

One day, I received a postcard from Robert, the Swiss man I met in London. In the postcard, he said he intended to spend a two week holiday in Tel-Aviv. He also said I should pay him a visit in the Hilton Hotel where he would be staying.

Before he sent me the postcard, I had received an earlier letter from him in which he said he had incurred a leg injury through a slight accident whilst skiing at a holiday resort, but he had since recovered from the injury.

I was a bit surprised that Robert communicated with me in Israel, because, when I gave him my address in London and he had said he would pay me a visit in Israel, I had taken it with a pinch of salt.

Robert's arrival in Tel-Aviv coincided with the time I was deeply involved, emotionally, with Moti Malkom. Although I paid him a visit at his hotel when he arrived, my mind was still with Moti Malkom.

I took him to Old Jerusalem and most of the tourist attractions. He bought me a few nice dresses. When he paid me a visit at home, my mother and some relatives of mine, who were always around the house, were very impressed with his appearance. He dressed very well and smoked expensive cigars. He expected me to be very close to him as I had been in London.

I impressed upon him that I was no longer the kind of woman he knew in London. I was now a changed woman, decent and respectable.

He replied by saying he had always known that. He added that the way I had treated him in London, spending the whole day taking him around and showing him places, was very unlike what he had with other women. My behavior toward him was more like a friend.

In spite of the fact that he was kind to me, and had very nice words for me, I had some arguments with him; he was complaining to me that he thought I was not nice to him. The main reason why I was not nice to him was that my heart was still with Moti Malkom. I saw it as an act of infidelity to go with someone else even though Moti was a married man.

Because of his disappointment with me, he telephoned to cancel his holidays by one week and arranged to leave Tel-Aviv prematurely.

When I told my mother about it, she was very annoyed with me because she felt a man like Robert would be good for me, and I would be stupid to terminate our relationship.

I agreed with her views when I thought about it. I went back to him and apologized. I convinced him to nullify the cancellation of the holiday and fix his date of departure as he originally planned. He agreed and did it that way.

One of the points that had been in his disfavor during the arguments was the fact that he was twenty-eight years older than I was, and he was a married man. Although Moti Malkom was also married, unlike Robert, I felt we had quite a lot in common.

At the end of his two week holiday, Robert left Tel-Aviv in the best of spirits, because, after the arguments, I became quite friendly and nice to him.

Not long after the ill-fated trio broke up, the telephone rang one night about 8.00 p.m. My mother answered it and said the call was for me. It was Pishon, the owner of the agency on the line. He wanted me to come and see him in his office in one hour's time. He had never telephoned me at home before, so I was very excited because I thought he must have a job lined up for me.

I hurried to the agency only to discover that I was mistaken. He had telephoned me in order to make love to me. When I arrived there, he put his hand around me and started to seduce me. As I protested, he told me that all the big female stars the agency handled had to give in sexually, otherwise, they would not have gotten anywhere.

I felt disgusted by his cold, brutal approach. I felt humiliated. I once had occasion to see his wife whom I thought was extremely pretty. I could not comprehend why he was not satisfied with her; instead, he seduced other women.

After that incident, I decided I would not have anything to do with the agency anymore. I got a letter of release, and I started looking for other agencies.

In the meantime, my affair with Moti Malkom continued. It had been going on for about a year. I had gotten used to him. One day, I missed his company so much that I wanted to see him. I did not want to telephone him, so I wrote a letter, which I gave to one of my stepsister's friends to drop in his letterbox. I did that because I reckoned if I posted the letter it may take about one or two days before it reached him.

At the time of writing the letter, it did cross my mind that his wife may see the letter, but I did not seriously think she would read his personal letters.

Moti Malkom came to my house the same day at about six in the evening in a nervous state. He said his wife had seen the letter and read it, after which, an intense argument had erupted between them, culminating in her leaving the house with their child to stay at her mother's place. He was very concerned because she had never left him before. He said he had to go to her mother's place to calm her down, but first, he had to think of a convincing story to tell her and her mother. I could not offer any help in that respect, although I apologized to him about carelessly posting the letter through his letterbox.

Later, I had no regrets over the whole rumpus when I discovered from his attitude that he did not seem to care about my feelings one iota. All his concern centered on his wife.

A couple of days after that, I telephoned his wife in a bid to calm her down because I had met her and talked to her a few times.

It became apparent from our conversation that her husband had told her that I forced him to go to bed with me. I was annoyed when I heard that. I told her that what he had told her was not true. In anger, I said he was not Allan Dillon, and that I should rape him. Later, when I saw Moti Malkom, he told me he told his wife that because he wanted to absolve himself and calm her down. After that, I saw very little of him. I was a bit irrational about the whole incident. I took it deeper than just losing a lover, I felt there was suddenly a large vacuum in my life.

To add to my depression, I had very serious arguments with my mother. My two stepsisters, who were aged about twelve and nine, caused the fact. They were in the habit of beating and shouting at my son, who was only six years old.

They were very rude to my son and me, telling us to leave the house because it was their father's. They were so disrespectful, that, at times, they used to hit my mother.

One day, out of curiosity, I decided to go to Jerusalem to see what was happening in my father's house. My stepsister, from my father's second wife, occasionally came over to Tel-Aviv and spent some time in my mother's house where she felt very much at home.

I had not seen my father for eleven years and thought he must have aged considerably.

When I saw him, the skin on his face had gone saggy. He did not display any emotions when he saw me; he also hardly spoke to me. I felt like a stranger.

My stepmother was more open and friendly with me. She suggested I left Jerom with her for about five days. I thought it would be a good idea to leave him there, as it would benefit him greatly if he felt some kind of family belonging.

During a conversation with my stepmother, she told me my father had become a very religious man, an event that put extra strain into her domestic routine, which meant more work for her. According to the Jewish religion, milky dishes were used only for dairy food and meat dishes only for meat.

While I was there, I noticed that my stepsister was not living at home, she was apparently sent to live in a farm called Cefar Hayarock; the place had teaching and boarding facilities. My stepmother did this because she was not taking any chances with my father, who, in spite of his religious conversion, may be tempted to tamper with her too. His religious devotion was a cover-up display. The man did not have even a small slice of conscience.

After about five days, I went back to Jerusalem to collect Jerom. He told me that my father had locked him up in a room because of a mischievous act he had committed, and he had gotten out of the room by climbing out of a window. It reminded me that, when I was with my father, I accepted everything that been dished out at me. I was too frightened of my stepmother and my father.

A few weeks after I visited Jerusalem, my father surprisingly paid my mother a visit in her apartment in Tel-Aviv after more than twenty years of not seeing each other.

In a way, it was weird to see these two people reunite, and I felt strange. I had never seen them together. The visit was a very short one. My father had come especially to ask if he could adopt and send my son, Jerom, to a religious school to train as a Rabbi. I was too frightened to let go of my son, fearing he would rape him too. He also said something that still puzzles me to this day, that was, "Why did you give your son your husband's family name? He should have be given my name," which was Toby.

I heard my mother talking to my father, warning him about being fair when it came to preparing his will. She told him, "Don't you forget, Ruthi and Debra are your flesh-and-blood daughters from God. You had better put them in the will and be fair to them." My mother was warning him, and my father was just nodding his head receptively in a concurring manner.

I discussed the issue of Jerom going to a religious school with my mother who was not terribly keen on the idea. My stepsisters had eavesdropped on our discussion. They went to Jerom and started mocking him about how ugly he would be as a Rabbi. They made fun of the way the orthodox men used to grow ringlets by the side of their ears. Jerom started to cry and begged that I should not allow him to go.

One early evening, my mother and her sister, in the company of a few neighbors, sat in the living room close to the balcony that had a large moving glass door. My stepsisters and I had one of those big fights where they went wild saying nasty things to me and hitting my son.

My mother always watched us without saying anything. It seemed she could not control these two little monstrous children of hers. She kept passive on that issue, and I felt like a stranger and an unwanted daughter in her house. She closed her eyes, not interfering with what was going on between my stepsisters, me, and my son, who was her first grandson. My son also felt that he had been treated unfairly, let alone without getting any affection or shown any care from my mother or any other family members. They were all a barbarian bunch of so-called "family." Jerom was much better off with my mother-in-law, where he had been educated with good English mannerisms and respect; they really loved him, they enjoyed having him in their house. It was painful for me to see my son having such hard times. He had to learn completely new languages. He was running wild in the streets most of the time, and on top of all that, being bitten and mocked by my two viscous stepsisters, who made me very upset and powerless to do anything to improve my son's comfort. The more I tried to talked to them or tell them off, the worse they became. On the other hand, my mother just used to shout, scream, and curse at them in Arabic. In fact, they were controlling her. They used to beat her and talk back to her in a rude manner. My mother was a lazy and fat woman whose life was dominated by gambling. She did not like to cook or clean her home and she even told me one time that she did not like children.

On this particular occasion, I was so upset at the way my stepsisters were carrying on that I asked my mother if it was fair for the girls to say we should leave the house. They were literally the bosses of the house. My mother replied by saying she thought the girls were right, the house belonged to them by virtue of the fact that it belonged to their late father.

Her answer was a very sad realization for me, especially when I thought of my neglected childhood, how she did not care about me then, and even as an adult, she still did not care. I felt she owed me something as a mother; it was so sad for me thinking I was going to be saved in Israel with my mother and Jerom, her grandson.

I felt I was a stranger even in my mother's home. I felt a feeling of utter helplessness. I had lost Moti Malkom as a lover, my mother had no love for me, and I had no money. The only person I had was my son, whom I had to take care of, and I was not doing a good job of it. I kept thinking repeatedly about the time Jerom was with my mother-in-law in England, he was well-educated with good manners, but my mother never showed any love and never cared about him. Jerom became wild and ill mannered like my stepsisters.

A combination of all these things made me think I had come to the end of the road. I had nothing to live for. I decided to stand on the edge of the balcony, knowing that a fall from there would mean instant death. I must admit, I was a bit theatrical about it; all I really wanted was for my mother to show some sign that she cared for me. How mistaken I was; that was asking for the impossible. She did not move out of her couch or care if I jumped down from the terrace or not. If anything, by her attitude of unconcern, she gave the impression I would be doing her a favor if I jumped down and died.

One of the neighbors who was sitting in the living room with her, came over to me, took me by the shoulder, and calmed me down with some kind words.

I decided after that incident that I would go back to England. I wrote a letter to Dadley in London and asked him if he would like me to join him. He replied in the affirmative.

I manage to bribe my mother for some money by telling her that the best thing for Jerom and me was to return to England.

I took a ship from Haifa to Marseille, France; from there I took a train to London.

My son had forgotten how to speak English; he only spoke Hebrew, which he became fluent in. Whenever I spoke to him in English, he always replied in Hebrew.

That, I thought, was a sad epitome of the kind of life I was living. For one reason or another, I could not allow my self to be settled; I stumbled from place to place, so my son had to suffer from the vagaries of my unsettled life.

CHAPTER ELEVEN

I

The train that brought me to London terminated in Victoria Station. With my son walking by my side, I carried our suitcases out of the platform, after which, I saw the handsome frame of Dadley walking toward us.

He gave me a kiss and carried the suitcases. I asked him where we were going to; he replied that we were going to stay at his mother's house in Seven Oaks. We took an underground train to Charing Cross from where we took another train to Seven Oaks.

His mother was a middle-aged lady who lived alone in a semi-detached house. She was a bit nervy when we arrived, but I guess she did not want to interfere in what Dadley, her son, did. She prepared dinner for us, which was comprised of pork chops and potatoes.

Jerom slept in the living room, while Dadley showed me a spare room on the second floor to sleep in. Later that night, Dadley came into my room expecting to make love to me. I was not quite ready for him, as I still did not have Moti Moghiyah out of my mind, so I told him, politely, that I was too exhausted from the journey.

I guess his pride had been hurt by my refusal. The next two days, I did not see him; he had left unceremoniously. His mother did not know where he was. I was lonely and bored those two days because Dadley's mother went to work in a school where she was a member of the catering staff.

On the morning of the third day, Dadley came back to the house with a girlfriend of his who was dressed in the outlandish clothes of a hippie. It appeared both of them had rehearsed between them how they were going to evict me from the house.

He said, in a belligerent tone, I must leave the house, while his girlfriend echoed the threat, although in a slightly subdued tone. He added that I was upsetting his mother and defaming his good name before her. During his two-day absence, I had told his mother that he was the father of my son Jerom, and that he was very irresponsible because he had shirked his responsibilities as a father when it mattered. I think his mother must have had a word with him about it. My initial reaction, when they asked me to leave, was to be stubborn. I said I had nowhere to go so I could not possibly leave. Nevertheless, their insistence on my leaving made me change my mind. The much-dreaded feeling of helplessness that had plagued me many times visited me again. I had no money and no friends I could go to for help. Rather than suffer in the streets with my son, I decided if the worst came to the worst, I was going to suffer alone.

I telephoned my mother-in-law in New Eltham and asked her if Jerom could stay with her again until I was able to stand on my feet and take proper care of him. Later that day, my father-in-law came over to the house, collected Jerom, and drove off very angrily.

With Jerom safely in the hands of my in-laws, I was a bit relieved, but that did not solve the dilemma of where I was going to stay. Dadley's resolve that I should go was unshakeable. I tried to beg, but it was like pouring water into a sieve, a fruitless enterprise. His girlfriend suggested she could take me to the Y.W.C.A. hostel where I would find temporary accommodation. I had no choice but to accept. On our way there, I was so bitter about the experience of being turned out of the house by Dadley, that I gave his girlfriend the letters he had written to me saying I would receive a good welcome, and that he would be very glad to see me.

His girlfriend took the letters from me very reluctantly and shrugged her shoulders as if to say, "Well, such is life."

I stayed in the hostel for two days, a pathetic, emotional wreck. On the third day, I decided to do something about my predicament.

If there was, anyone who could help me it was Robert in Switzerland. He had given me his son's telephone number in case I wanted to reach him urgently. He had a very close and special relationship with his son. I suppose since Robert was still living with his wife, it would have been too risky to give me his home number, so I decided to ring his son, who promised he was going to get in touch with his father and ask him to be present at his house to answer my call at a mutually convenient time.

I called at the pre-arranged time, and Robert was at his son's place to take the call. It was a reverse charge call. I told him about what had happened to me, and that I was homeless. He said I should take a train and come to Zurich, and he would be waiting for me at the station. Not believing my good fortune, I asked him what was going to happen when I arrived in Zurich. He replied by saying that I would be taken care of, and that I should just proceed to Zurich.

The money I had on me was just enough to take me to Zurich. The next day, I embarked on the journey. When I got out of the train in Zurich, I felt like a sojourner in a strange land. I was wary and unsure of myself. I wondered whether or not Robert would be in the station to welcome me. Apart from our meeting in London, and his subsequent visit to Israel, I hardly knew him very well as a person. I had accepted his invitation to come to Zurich not knowing what he had in store for me, not knowing what to expect. I wondered if his intentions were evil or altruistic.

As I walked toward the ticket barrier, I remember thinking to myself I was entirely at Robert's mercy. I spotted him as I handed my ticket to the ticket collector. He was a sight for sore eyes such as mine.

Although in his mid-fifties he looked a lot younger. He dressed sophisticatedly in a sports jacket, matching trousers, and at the end of beaming smile hung a fat cigar which he puffed very confidently. He was the picture of a God-sent man. He took my luggage from me, put it in the boot of his gleaming Mercedes Benz car, and asked me if I was hungry. I replied in the affirmative. He took me to a very posh restaurant where he treated me to one of the most expensive and delicious meals I had ever eaten.

I thanked him for the meal and more importantly for inviting me to Zurich. At that time, I did not really appreciate the fact that he liked me so much. I took things for granted. I was overtaken by events; I had no time for serious reflection and introspection. Robert told me he had taken two weeks off from work to go on holiday, and I was going to join him in this journey to Vienna. To say I was excited would have been an understatement. Having a holiday, when only a few hours before, my life had been bleak and so dreary, was simply incredible.

It was the month of November in the winter of 1972. The scenery as we drove from Zurich was picturesque, mountains and trees beautifully covered in snow. It was the first time in my life I beheld such beauty.

There were times I felt I was having a pleasant dream and feared that I was going to wake up suddenly to find it did not exist, except in my mind. It was reality alright, and I was part of it. Although our destination was Vienna, we took our time. Every now and then, after driving for about three or four hours, we stopped in a town, went to a restaurant to eat, and continued our journey.

Notable amongst some of these towns we stopped at was Innsbruck, where we spent the night in a three-star hotel.

The only unpleasant feature of the trip, for me, was what happened in the hotel that night. Robert went into the bathroom, brushed his teeth, put on his pajamas, and lay on the bed waiting for me to join him.

I remember going into the bathroom where I sat on the floor, ruminating on how good my relationship with him would be if I did not have to go to bed with him. I heard him call me several times while I was in the bathroom; I just sat there in a dejected mood. It was hard to believe Moti Malkom was still in my mind. He still had such a hold on me it was difficult to stop thinking of him.

My attitude toward Robert changed for the better when we arrived in Vienna. It took us two days to get there from Zurich. In Vienna, we checked into the Palace Hotel (reputed to be one of the best in town.)

We had a very enjoyable time in Vienna. He took me around to see places, we ate in the best restaurants, and he bought me a few expensive clothes.

Time seemed to fly as we enjoyed ourselves toward the end of the two weeks. We took our time in driving back to Zurich as we had done when we left.

Robert told me he was going to buy me a ticket to return to Israel as soon as we got to Zurich because he wanted me to think seriously over the commitment I was about to make, which was to share my life with him.

If I concluded that I wanted to share my future with him, he would send me a ticket to rejoin him and elaborate plans on how we were going to live.

In any event, he said he was going to mention to his wife and two children that he was going to invite a lady from Israel to Switzerland.

As he spoke, I had already made up my mind on what course of action I was going to take. I did not have to go to Israel to make up my mind.

I just had to learn to love him. Certain things were important to me. I wanted to live a peaceful life for a change. I felt I was wasting and unutilized. I could be useful to Robert. He reeked with confidence, knew what he was doing and where he was heading. He could build me up as a person and enable me to pick up the fallen threads of my life. I felt a large hollowness in me. I was vulnerable like a target set for practice shooting. Robert could protect me from the inhuman pellets of life. He would give me the sense of security I had lacked for most of my life.

Though I gave him an outright answer about wanting to share my future with him, he still insisted I went back to Israel and thought about it seriously instead of making any hasty decisions.

Reluctantly, I went back to the same old scene in Israel. My sense of pride was at its lowest ebb. I told my mother what was happening and that my son was with Brayen's parents. She thought leaving Jerom in England was a very good idea. In her opinion, he would get a very good education. My mother had no patience with children, and because she did not live an exemplary life, would have nothing to bequeath except bad things. She is not a good model to copy. Not only was she a compulsive gambler, she mixed with ill-assorted people, some of whom cheated her, fought with her, and were very rude to her.

I did not hear from Robert for awhile. I wrote him a letter, which I sent to his home address, inquiring about what was happening. Apparently, the letter had provoked a row between himself and his wife. Although he had told me in Vienna he would tell his wife and two children about me, he had not anticipated any trouble from his wife. From what I gather from him, because he and his wife had no form of sexual intercourse with each other for the past ten years, they merely shared the same house like strangers.

I received his reply in which he said I should not have sent the letter to his home address. However, he said after looking for an apartment for a few weeks, he had managed to find a suitable one in a village not far from his place of business. He owned a watch factory.

He also said that he had the opportunity to buy a house, but he thought it would be better to rent. Also in the letter, he wanted final confirmation that I wanted to live with him.

I received a letter back from him four weeks later in which he enclosed a flight ticket with instructions to meet him in Zurich.

II

A new chapter was opened in my life when I left Tel-Aviv and arrived in Zurich. This time, my presence in Switzerland was not to seek any humanitarian help, but in response to Robert wanting me for what I was as a woman.

He had given me time to think over the implications of wishing to spend my future with him.

Without any shadow of doubt in my mind, I had decided to deal with the problem directly. I had decided long before I arrived in Zurich to make the most of the opportunity. It was not an easy decision to make. It was with some considerable difficulty that I managed to ostracize the thought of Moti Malkom from my mind.

When Robert met me in Zurich, he took me to a place called Charmet, in the Canton of Grisson, where he owned a chalet that he and his family used as a weekend house. The chalet was high up in the mountains; the house had beautiful, hand-carved furniture made from light oak wood and from its windows one could see an artificial lake below that generated hydro-electricity.

We stayed in the chalet for a few weeks. Enjoying himself, Robert used to make a fire in his chimney even though he still had the central heating and double-glassed windows. During the day, we spent time looking for the right furnishings to buy for our prospective apartment. The few weeks I spent there were very memorable for me. I enjoyed every moment of it, and I showered him with a lot of kisses and affection as a gesture of my gratitude for his love for me.

He was very good at making cheese fondue, which he often prepared for me by the fireplace in the dining room. Our shopping for the household things we needed for our apartment was quite extensive. Robert sought my advice on most of the purchases. The choice of the king-size bed we bought, the wardrobe, dressing table, light furnishings, and kitchenware were mine. The only time he departed from seeking my advice was when we went into a furniture shop. He surprisingly let the female sales assistant who served us to influence his purchase. It did not surprise me that she convinced him to buy one of the most expensive sets of furniture.

Two weeks after we moved into our new Apartment in Nidau, I received a beautiful gold watch from Robert for my twenty-eighth birthday, which was on February 27, 1973. It was a Tiso, one-piece, eighteen-carat gold watch.

Funnily enough, I did not think much of the present at that time. Because he was a millionaire, my expectations were, perhaps, a bit too high. To me, the present was more like something a teenage girl from a rich family would get as a present. However, in later years, the design of the watch became very fashionable, and I grew to like it very much.

In April of 1973, Robert thought we should go somewhere for the Easter holidays. I suggested Austria because I had gone there with him before when I joined him from England, and I had thoroughly enjoyed myself on that occasion. I liked the sight of the snow-capped mountains and the beautiful winter scenery.

He agreed about going to Austria. We took the same pattern as our first trip there. We drove in his Mercedes for a few hours and stopped in the nearest town where we ate in a restaurant, and, at times, spent the night.

On our way to Austria, an odd incident happened when we were in Innsbruck. Robert and I were shopping and sightseeing when my eyes caught sight of a pair of sunglasses in a shop that catered for glasses. I told him I had seen a pair of sunglasses I liked and took him into the shop. When we got in there and looked at the sunglasses, we found that it had a Christian Dior trademark on it, and it cost two hundred and sixty Swiss francs.

I liked the sunglasses very much and thought they were good value for the money. Robert said he would not spend that kind of money on a pair of sunglasses, because, in his opinion, no sunglasses were worth that much; one was just paying for the Christian Dior trademark. Because I could not have them, I made a big thing out of it. Later that day, as we were driving out of Innsbruck, we had an argument about it. I was crying like a little, spoiled child and accusing him of not loving me and that was why he had not bought me the sunglasses.

He was livid with rage as he warned me to stop it. I think, to calm me down, he promised on our homeward journey that he would buy them for me.

Upon reaching Vienna, we stayed at the Palace Hotel for three days. One of the highlights of our stay in Vienna was when we went to a famous Hungarian restaurant where the waiters bowed down unusually low to us as if we were royalty. Robert explained to me that it was the traditional courtesy of the Hungarian people. It was an overwhelming experience for me.

During our homeward journey, we spent our first night in Salzburg where we had dinner. The next day, we passed through Innsbruck where I had seen the sunglasses, but Robert did not stop to buy them for me as he had promised.

That provoked my verbal attack on him again. After a brief stop in Liechtenstein, we returned to Nidau, where I resumed my normal routine of life. The first two months after I arrived followed almost the same pattern. On Saturdays and Sundays, I never did any cooking at all. We used to drive off to different lakes and towns and eat in very posh restaurants. We normally left early in the morning and came back in the evening. These weekend drives made me know various parts of Switzerland quite well.

I was an excellent house keeper for Robert I kept the apartment very clean. Across the street from where we lived, there was a big and new supermarket where I used to shop for food. Wanting to spoil Robert, I would buy the best of everything and even fruits or vegetables out of season, they were more expensive. I used to hear the key in the front door every day during lunch on the exact hour which was twelve o'clock. Robert would walk in and find the dining table topped with a nice table cloth silverware and plates, nicely arranged on the table. The food had just finished cooking and was ready to be served. The domestic work usually kept me busy until two o'clock in the afternoon; that was the time Robert used to go back to his factory. And after he had his glass of wine during his lunch, he relaxed with a cigar and browsed trough his daily newspaper, liking to find out details on the sporting events. From time to time, he used to give me his own opinion on political events that were happening in the United States.

Life and its routines were becoming too robotic and boring for me. I started to get friendly with a woman next-door neighbor who was Swiss-German each time I went to the laundry room. One evening, while Robert was proudly smoking his Cuban cigars and watching his usual French T.V. channel that I did not understand a word of, I asked him if we could invite the Swiss-German woman and her husband for a cheese fondue dinner. Robert did not like the idea; his reason was that they were Swiss-German and not French-Swiss. I was surprised to realize that discrimination existed between the Swiss.

My boredoms laid me to ask Robert if I could study and learn French in the afternoons. He impressed upon me, that first, I should learn to read and write English and have a very good grasp of English, which would provide the necessary basis for me to learn French. Robert spoke many languages; French was his main language.

I also had two hours a week of music lessons during which I tried to learn how to play the piano. When Robert separated from his wife, he left everything in his house for her. Amongst the things he left was a piano, which he had bought for his son when he was twelve so that he could practice and learn how to play. However, his son gave up playing, and nobody else used the piano. Because I was learning how to play, Robert demanded the piano back from his wife.

After living with Robert for two months, I received a letter from the police in Bern stating that I could not remain in Switzerland because I was not Swiss, and I had no valid visa to remain in the country.

I discussed my immigration problems with Robert, who advised me to tell the authorities I was a bona fide student, studying French, English, and Music. Because I told them that, I was given a further seven month visa to stay in the country.

My life remained relatively steady as my household routine and studies continued. However, beneath the thin layer of steadiness, lay deep-rooted feelings of insecurity.

Ruth Toby

Occasionally, I communicated by letter to my mother and kept her informed of any developments in my life. During the summer of 1973, she arranged to pay me a visit in Nidau, Switzerland. She arrived accompanied by my two stepsisters and an aunt of mine.

Their visit coincided with Robert's holiday, which was in the middle of July. As my son, Jerom, was also on holiday in England, we sent him a ticket to come over so that we could all go to Spain on holiday.

When Jerom arrived, we all flew to Spain. My mother paid the fares for my aunt, stepsisters, and herself, Robert shouldered all other expenses. We stayed in a holiday resort twenty miles from Bennidorm, where Robert rented a villa with a heated swimming pool, where my son and stepsisters had a great time. Robert also rented a car which we drove around to restaurants, to the sea, and other places.

Looking back, I guess I also had a good time. Although, and I do not know why, at that time, I did not really feel I was enjoying myself.

After the holiday, we returned to Switzerland through Barcelona. A few days after we arrived back, my mother left for America with my aunt and stepsisters. At the end of the summer holidays, Jerom returned to England to stay with my mother-in-law who was at the airport to collect him. Jerom also visited us every half-term, and on such occasions, he used to have a small, plastic bag tied round his neck where he kept his passport and other vital documents. The hostesses on the plane were always very kind to him.

When my visa to remain in Switzerland expired, I tried to renew it again, but this time, the authorities refused, despite the fact that I told them I was still studying.

I discussed the problem with Robert, who was very angry and complained to the authorities of how much tax he gave to them during all the years, and he also told them that I was his housekeeper. His letters to them were ignored. There was nothing he could do to alleviate it. I, therefore, decided to go to New York and join my mother until Robert and I could work something out. I got an entry permit from the American Embassy and flew to New York.

My mother was in Brooklyn, where she had rented a cheap apartment. My stepsisters, who were with her, were schooling in the neighborhood. When I arrived there, my mother was contemplating marrying an American in order to satisfy the immigration requirements to remain in the country. Nevertheless, fortunately for her, she met a lovely old pensioner who really liked her and wanted to marry her, not just for the convenience of staying in the country but as a permanent partner.

My stepsisters were against the idea of her getting married because they did not like the man as a stepfather; maybe because they thought he was too old.

I advised my mother to ignore their opinions about the man, because, in about five years' time, my stepsisters might leave the house when they get married themselves, and, as she was getting old, a husband and companion would be a valuable asset to her. She appeared to take my advice because they got married a few months later.

While I was with my mother, I met one of my female cousins who had been born in Israel but brought up in America. She was married to a divorced Jewish American. They owned a beautiful villa in an area of New York called Queens. When I paid them a visit one day, she seemed to revel at parading her wealth before me. She spent a long time telling me how many fur coats she owned and the value of her diamond rings.

By nature, I am not a jealous person, but she tried to make me one.

Within the short space of time I spent with them, it was apparent to me that she and her husband were compulsive gamblers. I had an unfortunate experience with them that emanated from this fact.

Whilst in their villa, I sat watching them as they played poker. They invited me to join them in what I thought was an innocuous game of poker. I joined them so as not to be antisocial. The experience cost me $100.00. I had to pay them with the traveler's checks I had with me.

Living in my mother's apartment in Brooklyn, New York was very different from the months I spent in Switzerland. The former typified abject poverty, while the latter, affluence. An unfair comparison, I must admit, but I had no choice in that matter. The apartment was stuffed with dilapidated, ugly, second-hand furniture. My mother had an almost morbid fascination with the color red. In fact, all the curtains in her apartment were bright red. However, in spite of this, I was relatively content with staying there. I adjusted myself rather quickly to the American way of life within only a few weeks after I arrived there.

I had very serious discussions with my mother about the possibility of my staying permanently in America in view of the precarious nature of what living in Switzerland would entail for me, especially with the immigration authorities.

I enrolled into an evening school, where I studied English. My English needed some polish.

My stepsister's friend, Hannah, who was spending some time with her stepsister in Brooklyn, used to taunt me about the evening classes, but that did not stop me from attending.

I also purchased a piano for $100.00 from my mother's husband, although they were not married then. He was very kind to my mother. He bought her a lot of clothes and many valuable things.

He displayed a lot of concern and affection for me, even more than my mother ever did. Maybe his attitude toward me was that way because I was instrumental to my stepsisters accepting him as a stepfather.

I received a few letters from Robert in which he expressed that he missed my company and wished I were with him in Switzerland.

On November 20, 1973, I got a pleasant surprise from him when he sent me a letter in which he said he had made elaborate plans for both of us to tour America.

According to the letter, he had booked the tickets through a travel agent in Switzerland, and my ticket was to commence from New York. I was overwhelmed by the thought of touring America; it was not everyday one had such an offer. I telephoned him that same day and gave my full blessing to the idea of the tour.

When he arrived in New York, I met him on 42nd Street where he was staying in a very expensive hotel. While I was with him in his hotel room, he told me in detail the various places we were going to tour. At the end of which, he surprisingly told me that, he had bought me a return ticket to go back to Switzerland with him when the tour was over.

177

This came as a shock to me. I was completely stupefied and lost for words. I had a fighting chance of beginning a new life in New York. His offer was so inviting and dazzling that I was not quite sure whether I had made the right decision or not. I replied after a few minutes saying I thought that I would like to remain in New York. On hearing this, his face became a mark of anger. I would never forget the expression he had on his face. He looked like an ageing actor playing the part of a villain.

The deep wrinkles in his face were accentuated as his face muscles creased in anger. With his greasy hair falling to one side, he asked, "So what have I come all the way from Switzerland to New York for?"

I became very apprehensive and replied by saying that I thought his invitation to tour America with him was borne out of the fact that he wanted to see America, as it was the first time he had been to the country. I did not realize there were strings attached to the offer, which was that I had to go back to Switzerland with him.

In any event, I told him I would think over the offer and give him an answer when I had come to the right decision.

The next day, the first leg of our tour started when we flew to New Orleans. I loved the city and thought that I would have liked to live there. I liked the banana trees, swimming pools, and nice villas by the sea. We stayed in a hotel not far from the Mississippi River. We visited lot of places including the French quarters in the town. We booked to see and have dinner in a club where one of my favorite jazz singers, Nancy Wilson, was having, to my surprise, a show. I am very critical about singers, but in my opinion, Nancy Wilson's talent put her in a class of her own. She struck me as having a rich theatrical side to her singing.

We left New Orleans for Salt Lake City where we saw, among other things, the church of the religious sect called the Mormons, which was not exactly my cup of tea. From Salt Lake City, we went to San Francisco, which we both loved. We stayed in a hotel adjacent to the terminus of the tramway bus. The picturesque sight of the bay littered with small boats, coupled with birds flying around, was a remarkable sight. We had a delicious meal in the Fisherman, a famous fish restaurant.

From San Francisco, we proceeded to Albuquerque, which we also enjoyed visiting. We hired a small plane and flew over the Grand Canyon. We visited Las Vegas where we gambled a bit. Robert, like me, was not keen on gambling. While in Las Vegas, we went to the Duns Hotel. There, we went to a big nightclub where Robert was thrilled by the sight of topless French dancers.

Though I had one of the best times of my life during the tour, I was still very reluctant to go back to Switzerland with him because of the uncertainty of my future in Switzerland. I had no form of security, and I let Robert know that. I had a conversation about all these things with my stepfather, who gave me the best advice of my life. He had explained to me that Robert was much too much older than I, and the only way for me to go with him, was to get married. He also told me that I should wait in New York until he was free of his wife. I told him that Robert had never begged me before the way he did, and that I had some feelings for him, and I should go back with him. "In this case," he said, "you had better ask him to prepare for you a life insurance of one million dollars." That is, until he was ready to married me. Robert promised me that one of the conditions he was laying down for me to go back with him was that, as soon as we went back, we would both go to a friend of his who was a lawyer and start divorce proceedings against his wife. If he got legally divorced, then the possibility of our getting married would be very feasible. And, in addition to that, he would prepare, in the meantime, the life insurance for me. By saying that, he was making me an offer I could not refuse. When we returned to New York, we both saw my mother, and I told her about the new developments. She did not try to make me change my mind, and I was so appreciative to my stepfather who saw my naivety and the timid nature in me. He had opened my eyes to the realities and securities of life by giving high values to me. He also planted the roots in my mind of how to grab opportunities and not let anyone take advantage of me. Robert and I flew back to Switzerland together.

In January of 1974, Jerom came over to Switzerland and the three of us went on our first skiing holiday together in a place called Arosa. We stayed in a nice hotel. During the first day of the holiday, we went into a sports shop where we tried out a few ski suits and shoes and ended up buying some of the equipment. Initially, I had some considerable difficulty walking in them. The ski resort was very crowded, and the activity there was frantic.

In the evenings after skiing out in the beautiful fresh air, we were so drained of energy that we could not go out to enjoy ourselves.

III

The discovery that, after I came back from America, Robert did nothing about his divorce with his wife as he had promised he would, provoked arguments between us.

I became increasingly worried about how reliable he was and how insecure I was. I had no financial problems with him, neither did I have the problem of food or where to stay, but the most important things I yearned for at that time were beyond my reach.

I wanted to be with my son, but that was impossible. He said he could not live in the same house with Jerom because he was savage and made him nervous. I had no husband. I was just his mistress whom he took to expensive hotels. Each time we went to a hotel, he booked in his own name while I booked in mine. That was not what I wanted. I wanted to be part of him, to be his wife.

Nevertheless, I could not be part of him, because, as his mistress, he was putting me at arms length. This made me have to rethink the stability and worth of our relationship. There were times the sad truth surfaced to my mind, realizing that just to have a place to live and food to eat was not enough to enrich my soul. I was bored. I did not have any friends. I did not understand the Swiss languages. I did not have any fun, and I was not happy. We should not have been together. If I had not been in need when I arrived in London on Dadley's invitation, I should never have bothered to get in touch with him. The fact that I was twenty-eight and he was twice my age, did not augur well for our relationship. He was set in his ways, he did not want me to have a baby, and the question of marriage had been delayed every day for all kinds of excuses.

I did not really love him, but I always lived in the hope that I would grow to love him one day. Sexually, he did nothing for me. I went to bed with him because it was more like an obligation to please him. For his age, he was very active sexually. I remember I used to keep a diary of how many times per week we made love together because he always accused me of not having it frequently with him and complained that I did not love him. To prove it to him, I used the diary as evidence of the frequency of intercourse with him.

The more I thought about my future with him, the more disenchanted I was with life.

If he had wanted to make me a star, it should have been within his reach to do so. If he invested some money in me and let me build a future as a singer because he knew I had talent it would have been something. But he was frightened that if I became a star, I would be self-sufficient and independent. Life would have been more meaningful for me if I had married him and had a child from him. I could be anybody's mistress but that was not what I aspired for in life. My entire life had been crazy. I had to draw the line somewhere.

By his own admission, he did not love me in the beginning, but he later fell in love with me. I appreciated that and thanked him for it, but what I wanted was a future. As far as he was concerned, he had no future ahead of him. He had played his chips in life. He was a fully realized man.

I told him repeatedly, that, unless he would get a divorce and marry me, I was going to leave him. A theme I hammered upon when I was in America while he was persuading me to come back to him.

Somehow, my mother-in-law got wind of the fact that I threatened to leave him. She had written two letters to Robert where she described me as a woman lacking of substance. She told him that I was cheap and irresponsible; degrading my name and saying I was not worth all the trouble.

She also wrote to me saying I should not commit the mistake of leaving Robert because I was his housekeeper whom he fed and paid. She saw me as a beast of burden, not as a human being with a mind, entitled to eke out a living in the way other normal people did.

Robert showed me the letters she had written to him. Maybe it was a bid to show he had nothing to hide from me, or probably, subconsciously, it was a way of telling me that she was corroborating his assessment of my worth. In any event, I bade my time and hoped for the best.

She had very good reasons to intrude into my life. I had gone to her twice when I wanted someone to take care of my son. That was a license for her to ride roughshod into my private life.

I should not have insisted on his getting a divorce from his wife if relations between them had been cordial. When I met him, he complained that they lived like strangers in the same house for ten years. The only connection they had was purely business. She managed one of the two floors of his watch factory. Maybe he felt if they got a divorce, his financial empire would crumble or he shirked threats very adversely.

I began to feel that, to him, I was just a young woman who was good in bed; a sex object he wanted to keep that way. Whenever we had a row over the issue of his divorce, I always slept alone in the little room Jerom used when he was on holiday. I did this to bring home to him the years when he used to live under the same roof with his wife but slept in separate rooms without having a sexual relationship. Occasionally, I also let him eat alone in his elegant dining room. He hated to eat alone.

One day, after I had another argument with him, I retired into seclusion in the little room. He asked me to join him in the sitting room where he was watching television. I refused.

I was so depressed, I got a bottle of tranquilizers I had from England when I separated from my husband. I took three of the pills, but it did not seem to be efficacious, so after a short interval, I took another four. I did this in an attempt to restore my emotional stability.

Robert came into the room asking if I was all right and returned to his favorite spot in the sitting room where he smoked his cigars. I sank into the quagmire of my confused thoughts, taking stock of my life, and wondering if I died whether Robert would feel any pity for me or not. I knew my father was too introverted and egotistical to care about what happened to me. As for my mother, she was too preoccupied gambling and seeking the pleasures of the world to care about a daughter she never loved.

Far more than anything else, the wicked words of my mother-in-law's letters kept reverberating in my head. I could not accept her assessment of me as a paid housekeeper. If she meant to destroy my ego, she achieved it. That night, I ended up taking about fifteen pills. I wanted some peace. I hoped I would achieve that peace in sleep, even if it meant sleeping forever.

I was drowsy and hovering between unconsciousness and consciousness. I remember at that juncture, Robert walked into the room. I told him how many pills I had taken. He thought I was joking and accused me of lying. He started playing with my nipples, trying to arouse me sexually.

I knew what the consequences of taking an overdose of drugs were, so I told him to take me to the hospital. He hesitated because he feared his prestige and reputation was at stake if it transpired that there was nothing serious happening to me. He finally decided the decision whether to go to a hospital or not was mine. If I wanted to go, I could go.

I slept for the next twenty-four hours until I was strong enough to continue my routine. I accused him of not caring. While I lay half dying, he was obsessed with playing with my nipples.

CHAPTER TWELVE

I

Robert and I had a very limited social circle. Our friends were very few. The only visitors we had were Bery, Robert's younger son, and Franswa, who was one of the two Swiss men I had first seen Robert with in the club in London. I never had the opportunity to meet the other man who was with them.

At the early stages of living with Robert, I gathered his wife told his two sons not to, under any circumstances, have any dealings with him, and to also try as much as possible to avoid coming to the apartment where their father and I lived.

After about two months, Bery seemed to ignore his mother's advice and visited us quite frequently. We used to eat cheese fondue together which his father prepared.

Franswa was working as an agent at a reputable Swiss insurance company, was about forty-five years old, and a bachelor. Sometimes, during some weekends, he used to accompany us when we crossed the border to France on a drive. I liked those weekend trips when we used to drive to several places; they helped in no small way to get me out of the drudgery that typified my weekdays.

For sometime, as early as when I was living with Brayen, my ex-husband, in London; I had some ear problems that impaired my hearing slightly. I went to a hospital, but the National Health Service could not do anything for me. I could have had treatment from a private doctor, but the expense would have been too much for me to bear. When I left London for Israel, my stepmother, who was aware of my affliction, told me that my father, who had malignant ear problems, had gone to a modern hospital in Tel-Hashomer, which was not far from Tel-Aviv. After the treatment, according to her, his hearing ability had increased tremendously. She suggested I went to the same hospital.

As it turned out, I did not get around to going to the hospital because the time I could have had the treatment coincided with my going to Switzerland. Coupled with the ill timing, Robert had told me not to worry about it because he reckoned I would have a better treatment in Switzerland.

True to his words, I saw a doctor in Bern who operated on the left ear in February 1974 and promised to do the same on the right ear six months later in September.

I was very restless one night just after I came back from the first ear operation. I could not sleep because the thought of being with my son and the lack of security in my life were recycling in my mind. I sat on the toilet where I began to cry.

My crying must have woken Robert, who inquired about the cause of my despair. I told him I missed Jerom, and I wanted to be with him. He said I saw him quite often during the half-terms and when he was on holidays, which was reasonable enough. However, he added, if I wanted to go to London to see him over the weekend, he would provide me with the tickets for the journey. That act of kindness relieved me like a tonic.

The next morning, the necessary arrangements for my trip to London were being arranged. I planned to take Jerom to stay with me in the Hilton hotel in Park Lane opposite Hide Park, and then return him to my mother-in-law when I was ready to come back.

The trip to London was a revelation for me. It told me more than anything else could, that if I was not prudent enough in my dealings with my mother-in-law, she may be unwilling to ever give my son back to me again. Though I did not give her any financial assistance for looking after my son, I always ensured, without fail, that Jerom would have the best clothing and toys whenever he was going back to London after holidaying with me; I also sent her very expensive presents. I did that in appreciation of the service she was rendering to my son and me. In any case, I decided to speak to a lawyer about custody proceedings for my son. I left my address with him so that he could get in touch if there was any development over the issue.

The short time I spent in London was most enjoyable for Jerom and me. I took him shopping and bought him whatever he wanted. We went to nice restaurants; we walked in the Hide Park. Jerom had a lot of fun and he was very happy.

When I returned to Switzerland, I decided I was not going to sit on the fence and wait for things to happen, I was going to try to establish a more solid relationship with Robert.

From my experience in life, when a woman really wants a man who is either undecided as to what to do or who is playing hard to get, the strategy the woman often employed was to get pregnant from him. My mother once hinted subtly to me something along those lines.

I made up my mind I was going to adopt the same strategy of getting pregnant with Robert. I figured out if I was carrying his baby, he might do something about his divorce. I, therefore, ignored the pill. After six weeks without seeing my monthly menstrual period, I was sure I was pregnant.

One afternoon, when he came home for lunch, I broke the news to him. He was so dumbfounded that he could not help but think I had gone out of my mind. He asked me if I had gone crazy. His exact words were, "Do you want to suffer all your life?".

The meaning and implication of those words were not lost on me. I felt more insecure by his revelation of how he felt about my getting pregnant. It crossed my mind that he probably did not love me at all.

Before he returned to work that afternoon, he insisted that I must have an abortion.

In the evening, when he came back from work, he reiterated his insistence on my procuring an abortion. Because of the hostility that was implicit in his reactions, I told him that if he wanted me to have an abortion, he should give me 30,000 francs for toying with my life and the time I spent with him. I told him he used me like a sex object to gratify his sexual hunger whilst he pretended to love me. I thought if he gave me the money that would compensate me and set me on the road on my own. At that juncture, I remembered succinctly one of the few pieces of advice my mother once gave me. She said when a young woman lives with a rich old man whose selfish interests predominate over all other issues, the young woman should try to get as much as possible out of him. I was that young woman.

I told him directly that if he did not want to father the child and insisted on an abortion that was proof he did not love me, and I would have to leave him to start life afresh again.

Living with him had transformed my standard of living; my hitherto simple life had now become sophisticated. I lived in luxury, visited the best hotels, and drove about in a Mercedes Benz.

The psychological implications of falling from the dizzy heights of good living to the depths of subsistence living would be too traumatic for me. I told him I asked for the money because I wanted to go to America and live with my mother. He agreed he was going to give me the money. To me, that was like turning a knife in my wound. It hurt me very deeply. I could not quite rationalize why he was ready to part with so much money just to make me procure an abortion.

His uncaring attitude drove me to the extreme of getting hard and demanding money from him. That was the only way I felt I could redress the balance.

The next day, during his lunch break, he handed me 15,000 francs and promised to give me the balance after the abortion. When I demanded the full amount, he complained bitterly that I had no iota of trust in him. However, he managed to convince me to wait until after the abortion.

Before I went to a hospital to see a gynecologist, I put the money in a bank. After the doctor examined me, he told me that I was not pregnant. The doctor said, it frequently happened that when a woman suddenly stopped taking the pill, changes often occurred in her menstrual period. My case, in the doctor's opinion, was one of such cases.

I went back home and told Robert what had happened. I told him in spite of what had happened, I still wanted the 15,000 francs he was supposed to give to me so that our relationship could be terminated. He argued he could not give it to me because I was not pregnant, and when he suggested I was trying to blackmail him, I let the matter die a natural death. My plans to go to America remained unchanged.

I went to the American Embassy and got an entry permit. Robert bought a ticket for New York that enabled me to stop in London for a few days as a transit passenger. The reason for this was to afford me the opportunity to see Jerom. I had no idea how long it would take before I saw him again.

According to my plans, when I got to America, I would try and get settled. After that, I would send for Jerom to join me.

Because of a row I had with my mother-in-law over Jerom, I had to leave for New York earlier than scheduled. I wrote a letter to Robert when I got to Brooklyn.

About two weeks later, I got a lengthy reply from him in which he said he could not do without me, and I should return to Switzerland as soon as possible. He also said he would do something about his divorce. At the end of the letter he expressed the view that if I agreed to go back to Switzerland, we would go somewhere on holiday, preferably to London to see Jerom.

I thought that he must have had a rethink about the way he treated me and had decided to take me more seriously. I made up my mind I would give myself another chance and go back to him.

When I flew back to Switzerland, we arranged with Franswa, his only friend, and a girlfriend of his, to go to Nice in France on holiday in two weeks. However, before the trip, Robert arranged for us to go to London and see Jerom for a few days as he had promised we would do in the letter he had sent to me in America.

We stayed in the Hilton Hotel with Joe for five days. As usual, we bought him several presents. Robert and I seized the opportunity to see the lawyer who was handling my son's custody and tried to make him get the case moving.

A week after we flew back to Switzerland, we left for France with Franswa and his girlfriend. We stayed in Nice for only five days. While Robert and I thoroughly enjoyed ourselves, Franswa and his girlfriend had arguments most of the time. He alleged she did not allow him to make love to her, and Franswa felt bitter about it, having paid her fare to Nice. He felt at least he deserved some love in return.

Not long after we returned from Nice, I received a letter from Lenna, my stepsister's friend in Israel. In the letter, she said she was coming to spend some time with me. Shortly after that, she flew over to Switzerland.

Because of her presence in the house, Bery stayed around more often. Lenna behaved very badly. She refused to eat with us at the same table; she always complained, asking me to leave her portion in the oven until she was ready to eat. She not only talked to me disrespectfully, she also conducted herself as if her presence in the house was a right and not a privilege.

After a few days' stay, she seemed to like Bery who often took her out.

Jerom came over to spend his summer holidays while she was still there. We arranged to go to Israel together for a vacation. When we got to Israel, we parted company with Lenna, who went back to her parents while we stayed at the Hilton Hotel in Tel-Aviv for two weeks.

I felt good going back to Israel and staying in a posh hotel like the Hilton. We rented a car and drove to Jerusalem where we stayed in one of the best hotels there.

Whilst in Jerusalem, I telephoned my father's house and spoke to my stepmother. I asked her if it would be alright if Robert, my son, and myself paid them a visit. She said it would be perfectly alright.

My father had never seen me with a man before. I was a little bit apprehensive about what his reactions would be. When we arrived at his house the next day, he was not around. My stepmother said he had gone out. I suspect he went out deliberately to avoid us.

However, we arranged to take my stepmother and my stepsister, Yemet, who was on vacation from Hacfar Hayarok, for a drive the next day to Old Jerusalem.

The next day we drove to Old Jerusalem as planned. We went to a restaurant where we had Arabic food. Throughout our stay in the restaurant, Robert completely ignored me. His undivided attention centered on my stepsister. I had an argument about it with him later and told him maybe I had suddenly become too old for him and he preferred my stepsister for that reason.

That was not the only occasion during the holiday when he had ignored me over some other woman. During our flight back to Switzerland, he sat next to a Swiss woman, and he engaged in a conversation with her during most of the five hour flight. At the end of the journey, I accused him of ungentlemanly conduct. He told me naively that he did not want to disturb me and that was why he had not spoken to me. And secondly, he had a very interesting discussion with the Swiss woman about how savage and primitive the Israeli people were. I was so annoyed I asked him if they were so savage and primitive, why he had anything to do with me. I made an issue over it for some time. Each time it provoked an argument.

II

In the September of 1974, I had my right ear operated on by the same doctor who had done the left one six months earlier. After the operation, I asked the doctor if he could recommend a plastic surgeon to carry out an operation on my nose.

I had the shape of my nose slightly altered when I was in London because of a complex I had about it. It looked too much like my father's nose.

The doctor recommended two plastic surgeons that he said were very good. When I came back home, I tried to convince Robert to finance the cosmetic operation on my nose, because, from a beauty point of view, the operation I had in London was a disaster. He agreed and I was very pleased with the outcome.

Three months later, Jerom came over to Switzerland for the Christmas holidays. When he was due to go back, I cancelled his flight to London because I decided I wanted him to stay with me.

I wrote a letter to my mother-in-law disclosing my intention. She replied saying if I did not send Joe back, she was going to write to the Swiss police telling them that I was abducting Jerom.

She knew my circumstances in Switzerland and that the Swiss police may take a dim view on my wanting to live there with my son. She knew I was vulnerable. I was not prepared to give in easily. I decided if I took Jerom to Israel, there was nothing she could do to make me return my son to her. Therefore, I flew to Israel and stayed with Lenna in Tel-Aviv.

I received a letter from Robert a week later saying he had heard nothing from the Swiss police, and he did not think my mother-in-law reported the matter to them. He suggested I returned to Switzerland.

After spending only sixteen days in Israel, I decided to return to Switzerland.

Because of my immigration problems, which meant I could not remain in Switzerland, Robert suggested I returned to England. Bery, Robert's son, once took an English course in Bournemouth, which proved worthwhile. He, therefore, suggested I took Jerom with me and studied English there.

I took his advice and returned to England. When I arrived, I informed my mother-in-law that I was staying in Bournemouth with my son.

We stayed in an inexpensive bed and breakfast in Boscombe, a small town next to Bournemouth, for a week before we got an apartment. The apartment rented as a holiday apartment, which I agreed to have from January to June, before I would give it up for holidaymakers.

I enrolled into the School of English and got Jerom into a local school.

While I was in Bournemouth, I met an Israeli couple who owned three houses, which they rented out as bed and breakfast accommodation. I got on very well with them, and, quite often, they invited me to their home.

I settled in Bournemouth, and I wanted a piano to practice on, with a view of improving my playing ability. I asked a boy from Thailand who was in my school if he knew where I could purchase a second-hand piano. Through his help, I got one. He asked me if he could come to my apartment and play on it at times. I had no objections whatsoever. One night, when I was speaking to Robert on the telephone, I told him in passing about the boy from Thailand. A few days later, I got a reproachful letter from Robert accusing me of infidelity and saying I should not dare invite a boy alone to my apartment. He said there was nothing like a platonic relationship between a man and a woman. A few more letters followed on the same theme in spite of my assurance to him that the boy was innocent. Besides, I told him he was not the type of person that would interest me. It took several weeks before he finally dropped the subject.

I got a surprise visit from Robert one night when I answered my doorbell and saw him standing outside the door. He had driven all the way from Switzerland. Although he told me he wanted to give me a surprise, I think the real reason for his unannounced arrival was he suspected I was cheating on him by inviting a man to my apartment. In any event, that did not spoil his visit. In the next few days, we drove to New Forest, Swanage, and the neighboring towns and villages.

In the middle of May, Jerom and I were on vacation for the half-term so we went to Switzerland where we accompanied Robert to a village near Fribourg and had a very enjoyable time. Our arrival in the village coincided with a festival for bands where it was full of pomp and pageantry.

The fun of the holiday did not last long, after returning to Switzerland, to our home in Nidau, which was next to Biene, or Bill in German, I realized that after more than four months since I returned to England, Robert was still his lukewarm self. He still rested on his oars neither making any short-term or long-term plans about our future. He let the relationship remain unchanged as if time was a meaningless concept that had no bearing on our lives.

In June, when I finished my studies in Bournemouth, I took Jerom with me to Switzerland where I hoped Robert and I would work out something about what we would do next. While we were there, he made elaborate plans for Jerom to attend a boarding school somewhere in the mountains.

By special arrangement, the parents of about twelve children, most of whom were foreigners, put them in the care of a family on a farm where the children lived together, socialized, and attended the school in the village. It was very expensive, and Jerom seemed to like the idea of going there. Before we did any arrangement to register Jerom into the school, Robert suggested we went to Italy on vacation.

Our first stop in northern Italy was in a seaside town called Pesaro. We had a good time there. The only unpleasant feature was at night when we could not sleep because of the noise made by people enjoying themselves.

From Pesaro, we left for a luxury holiday resort in Rosa Marina in the south of Italy where we had a rented villa all to ourselves. Four swimming pools, five restaurants, and a discotheque that played live music at night were some of the numerous facilities we had at our disposal.

During the first day of our stay, we had a tennis teacher who taught us how to play lawn tennis. Later, we were joined by an Italian woman who was with her daughter, a very attractive girl of about sixteen years. She often walked about clad provocatively in a bikini, which showed off her well-tanned body.

One day, Robert and I met her outside a supermarket, and to my surprise, Robert stretched out his head very noticeably toward her and peered down her brazier. His behavior was very embarrassing, although she seemed unperturbed about it. When we arrived back at the villa, I told him off for behaving so uncouthly. He denied he was peering down her brazier, and he did not think there was anything wrong with his behavior. The next day, when we went to play tennis, we met the young woman and her mother again. I played with her on one court, while on another court, Robert played with her mother. After a few minutes, Robert interrupted play and said he wanted to play with the young woman and suggested I play with her mother. His admiration for her was so blatant that I became infuriated. I banged my tennis racket on the court and returned to the villa. I walked around the villa wondering what to do to hurt his feelings the way he was hurting mine. I saw his packets of cigars, which I took into the bedroom. I removed the top sheets from his bed, tore the cigars, and spread the tobacco all over his bed. Then, I went into the kitchen and got some salt, which I spread over the tobacco. To crown it all, I got a kettle of water and poured it on the bed over the tobacco. The mess was my way of retribution for his behavior. He had invited me on what was supposed to be a holiday, but no sooner does he see a beautiful girl than he loses his cool.

Too frightened to be around when he discovered the mess on the bed, I went out with Jerom for a few hours. I returned to the villa to find him fuming with rage. He said I was irrational in destroying his cigars. He was unable to find that kind of cigar in that part of Italy, and he was going to punish me for my misbehavior by canceling our proposed trip to Yugoslavia.

I apologized and tried to make him change his mind but to no avail. After that, we were fighting continuously. Since our fights spoiled the fun of the holiday, I told him I would rather return to London than go back to Switzerland.

A few weeks before we embarked on this fighting-riddled vacation, Lenna had told me in one of her letters that she was in London staying in an apartment she had rented. With the knowledge that I could stay with her before I got a place of my own, I told Robert to drive me to her address when we got to London.

When we arrived there, contrary to what she had told me about renting the flat, we discovered she was only taking care of it on behalf of some friends who had gone abroad. Realizing that it would be an inconvenience to stay there in view of the circumstances, I tried to persuade Robert to take me back to Switzerland. He was furious at the suggestion and retorted by saying he had not driven all the way to London for nothing. He left me in the apartment and returned to Switzerland.

I stayed with Lenna for a short while, while looking for a flat, until I found one in northwest London, which was in the same area. It was a very expensive, but inadequately furnished flat, which I had intended to share with another girl. At the last minute, she disappointed me, so I had to take it alone.

I wrote to Robert keeping him up to date on all the developments since he left me in London, and we decided to forget about the arguments and rows we had had. As he did when I was in Bournemouth, he continued to support me. Every two or three weeks, he used to spend his weekends with me.

In June, my mother paid me a visit on her way to America. She had been holidaying in Israel. When I met her at the airport, my first impression was that she was dressed very cheaply. She wore a necklace with dangling, large coins that looked like imitation jewelry. Then, later, she told me they were gold, and that was how she took money out of Israel. She sold the coins at exorbitant amounts in America.

Her visit was not a very happy one in any sense of the word. I never took her out to see any places or shows, and because she spoke with a high tone, I always told her to moderate her voice. I reminded her of how badly she had treated me as a child and accused her of not loving me. She cried as I told her these things. At the end of her short stay, she bought so many things for my stepsisters and aunt that she ran out of money. She asked me to lend her twenty pounds to pay for excess luggage. I was very annoyed because I knew she might not pay me back because she always squandered her money gambling. When we got to the airport, she had to pay for her excess luggage as she had rightly anticipated. I gave her twenty pounds, adding that I wanted it back as soon as possible. Without saying goodbye, I left her and returned home. My childhood reminiscences were brought to the surface by her visit and left a dark cloud of sadness that hung around in my every thought, word, and deed. This dark cloud was partially dissipated, when, a couple of weeks following her departure, Robert sent two tickets for Jerom and I to join him in Switzerland where we would go on a skiing holiday.

We accepted the invitation and joined him in Nidau. Shortly after, we left for Montana, for a ski resort in the Canton of Valace. The resort had an ill reputation for being very warm, and, as it turned out, there was not enough snow to ski. In any case, we made the most of the holiday in spite of the unfavorable weather conditions.

Toward the end of the holiday, I had a nasty accident, there was not enough snow on the ground when I fell off the ski lift and ruined my ski suit in the process. Through the help of Franswa, who was in the insurance business, he took the insurance company concerned to part. They paid for a new pair of ski suits six months later. In the meantime, Jerom and I returned to London after the New Year celebrations of 1976. We had spent about three weeks in Switzerland.

In addition to my studies in English and learning to play the piano, I managed to devote some time to taking driving lessons. I spent about eight hours every week driving.

In my attempt to do something worthwhile with my life, I got membership to a club called Star Finder run by a singer with a classical music upbringing. All sorts of artists and entertainers were attracted to this club because it was a kind of melting pot where representatives from television, radio, and agencies hunted for talent. One of the conditions for membership was the ability to sing or entertain. When the person who ran the place heard me sing, he thought I was good enough to enroll as a member. He encouraged me and gave me a few lessons to improve on my technique. I used to sing in the club once a week. During one of Robert's visits, I took him there.

When I was singing, my eyes were always on him, but it was an ego-shattering experience, because the expression on his face was a melancholy one. It was not because I could not sing, but as he had told me many times, a singer's life was like that of a gypsy and he was not prepared to put up with it.

In the Easter of 1976, we went to the north of Italy on holiday by the lake of Lagardo. We enjoyed this holiday very much. Toward the end of the year, we also went on another ski holiday in Zermatt, a very beautiful village with snow-capped mountains. Unfortunately for me, a cold and bronchitis marred what could have been a fantastic holiday for me.

III

As usual, Jerom and I flew to Zurich for our Easter holidays by Robert's invitation. The next day after we arrived in Nidau, we left for Albergo in Italy. We spent a couple of days there before we left for Venice. It was my third time visiting that beautiful and remarkable city. We also spent a couple of days there before we went to Milano where we stayed in a hotel called Plaza Albergo. We came back to Nidau after a thoroughly enjoyable holiday, after which, Jerom and I came back to London.

Although I had some very good times with Robert, traveling to places and living quite comfortably, I also wanted, as I had always told him, the security of marriage. He often avoided this commitment. He continuously toyed with me when it came to his getting divorced; he did not even try. That made me very impatient with him. When I first lived with him, he told me he would like to retire before he was sixty. Later on, after I had returned to London, I suggested he spent his retirement in London with me if he was not willing to do something about his divorce.

In view of the fact that I could not live permanently in Switzerland, I suggested he bought a house in London. If he sold his chalet in Switzerland and gave half the proceeds to his wife, he could buy two houses here in London. He refused and gave me a stupid excuse that if he bought me a house, I would probably leave him in preference for a younger man.

I replied by saying he could have it in his name and see a solicitor to draft an agreement stating that if anything happened to him, the house would be mine. Initially, he agreed to my suggestion, but he later changed his mind and gave the excuse that he did not like to be in England, he preferred Switzerland. I was disappointed over it and had a very intense argument with him.

He said he did not intend to leave his work, as he did not think his son was capable of managing his watch factory. He ate his earlier words about retiring and said he was not going to rush anything.

I was sick and fed up with his tactics of providing finance for maintenance so that I could feel dependent on him. I told him I was not a commodity that he could buy, that indebtedness had amputated my freedom, and I had to dance to the tune of his music. He did not want me to become a singer; he also frowned upon making friends, whether male or female. He expected me to wait for him every two or three weeks when he came on weekends and made love to me a few times. Even a hermit would not cherish that kind of existence.

His manly, selfish interests were so overpowering that they blinded him to the fact that I was a human being with feelings, who deserved a normal life, and that I deserved to have future with commitment. I did not feel secured and I definitely did not want to be, or feel as though I was a private whore to him or anybody. Just because a person has money, it does not mean that he can do with me what he wants. I began to conclude that perhaps my testimony of love to him made no impact on him.

I tried to analyzing him psychologically as a means of understanding what made him tick. He was a man who had a very strange relationship with his wife before they separated. He was also a man, who, by his own admission, went around with prostitutes. From these two facts, I began to draw the inference that perhaps he saw a lasting relationship between himself and any woman as an unattainable feat.

Women, to him, in the words of an old saying, were "a necessary evil." His younger son, Bery, once told me that his father tried to pressure him into sleeping with a prostitute. He had numerous conversations with him where he denigrated the species called "women." It came as no surprise when Robert told his elder son not to get married to the woman that later became his wife, unless she signed a contract which stipulated that, in the event of a divorce, she would not be entitled to his part of the family fortune because she did not come from a rich family.

Because of my lack of confidence in Robert making up his mind about our relationship, I decided I was going to look for another man as a form of insurance, in case he turned out to be unreliable. I did not intend to rush it; rather, it was going to be a gradual process. I hoped to achieve this not by using my charm to entrap just any man, but to register myself with a computer dating service in London that would attempt, on the basis of the personal information I would give them, to find me a suitable man.

In May 1977, Robert did not want to take me with him on his next trip. He and his friend, Franswa, went on a vacation trip around Asia visiting places like Thailand, Hong Kong, the Philippines, and other countries. When he left Asia, he came straight to London where he gave me a box containing a lovely ring with a lot of small diamonds and three rubies. I was so excited about the present, I thought it was my engagement present. It turned out it was not.

The following month, Jerom and I went to Switzerland for one week. While we were there, a very odd incident happened. One evening, Robert was browsing through the pages of a T.V. magazine, his attention held for a long time by something he was reading. I asked him what it was, and he said it was an advert by a marriage bureau which guaranteed to get their clients marriage partners. I told him sarcastically that since he would not marry me, why he would not find me a husband. He said he should look into it during his lunch break the following day. He had often told me, if I left him, to use his words: "I would never find a man like him." His wealth gave him a lot of confidence. Maybe by agreeing to help look for a husband for me, he was confident I would never find a man as rich as himself, and having failed in accomplishing that, I would see him in a fresh light as being indispensable.

At that time, I had no idea that he was playing a game with me, but with the knowledge of hindsight, it was not difficult to see things in their true perspective. Naively, I played his game with him. The next day, during his lunch break, he arranged an appointment for a representative of the marriage bureau to take my biographical details, my interests, ambitions, and type of man I was looking for.

During the last two days of the holiday, I walked into a shop where I wanted to buy a pair of sunglasses I liked. The female assistant who was serving me could not speak English, so she called her boss, who was the owner, a young Swiss man in his early thirties who spoke English. He spent a few minutes talking about the merits of the glasses I wanted. After that, I changed the subject, and we discussed, freely, the Swiss people and their mannerisms. He was very friendly and offered to give me the sunglasses as a gift, but I insisted on paying for them. As I was about to leave the shop, he asked me if he could buy me a coffee in a nearby café the next day. After a slight hesitation, I agreed to meet him an hour after Robert's lunch break. The young man's name was Pranty.

I was very nervous about meeting Pranty the next day because Biene was a very small town, and maybe because Robert was a rich man, someone who knew both of us could see me and cause trouble, or Robert himself could, not to mention his two sons.

To minimize the risk of be seen when I met Pranty, I told him rather than sit outside, I preferred sitting inside the café. I had a very interesting conversation with him. He offered to show me around Switzerland, but I declined the offer. I told him about Robert, and that I had seen most of Switzerland. I also declined going out to a disco or a meal with him. I told him if he could come to London, I would show him places of interest there. Pranty felt sorry I had to go back to London the next day. He promised he was going to arrange for a weekend visit to London with a travel agency and would keep me posted about his date of arrival. I was quite enthralled about meeting him and looked forward to when he would come to London.

At that time, in the back of my mind, I was not sure if I was doing the right thing or not. On the other hand, I had a good excuse; to my way of thinking, the fact that Robert paid more than four hundred francs to a marriage bureau to find me a husband showed me the limits he could go to. The strange thing was that I did not know why he was suddenly doing that. It did not registered in my mind that perhaps he was trying to get rid of me for one reason or another. I also, at that time, naively thought that as a father figure, he cared about my future and me. Nevertheless, I was deeply hurt and humiliated by this attitude, and I was not suspicious of anything.

Three days after I went back to London, one of my stepsisters in America called Nadeia accepted an invitation from me to spend her summer holidays and come over to London. A couple of days after she arrived, Pranty also arrived from Switzerland. I had a very hectic time trying to ensure both of them a nice time. I took them to the several tourist attractions in London. I also took Pranty to visit Lenna, who was still in London, and together we went to a wimpy bar and several other places.

Pranty stayed in a hotel, but I invited him to spend a night with me. When he tried to make love to me, I was surprised to find him sexually weak, perhaps impotent. That fact put me off of him a bit, but I still cultivated his friendship and thought he was a very nice person.

A week after Pranty returned to Switzerland, Jerom, Nadeia, and I went to Switzerland to spend the summer holidays. Robert arranged that we went to Italy for two weeks. We went to Pescara, where we rented an apartment close to the sea. During the day, we swam, and Jerom had a great time collecting seashells from the shores of the sea.

One evening, we heard a piercing screams from Nadeia. She came upstairs and complained Jerom had punched her very hard on her tummy. Jerom said she had persistently taunted him. She had asked him for a fight, and when he refused, she had hit him, so he had no choice but to reciprocate. I told my stepsister, Nadeia, that Jerom was no longer that little child who, when we were in Israel, she and her sister used to beat him up all the time; where, at the end, she and my other stepsister, then only little children, influenced our mother to throw us out of my mother's house. I kept explaining to her that those days were gone. When Jerom came upstairs, she sprang on him again, and Robert and I intervened and kept her away from Jerom who was avoiding her. I ordered Nadeia to go to her room and stay there. She kept yelling and screaming in her room the whole night, and we were all disgusted by her behavior. Robert accused me of spoiling the entire holiday by bringing my stepsister along. I secretly sent a postcard to Pranty, telling him I was in Pescara, and I was coming back to Switzerland. I would see him before I returned to London.

When we returned to Switzerland, I took Nadeia with me to Pranty's shop. Pranty noticed she wore glasses and offered to give her contact lenses, which he did. At that time, they had just come out to the market, and they were very expensive. Nadeia was very pleased about it. I warned her not to mention it to Robert. Twice, in the company of Nadeia, Pranty and I went to a disco. On both occasions, I gave Robert an excuse to leave the house because I wanted to entertain Nadeia, and her holiday was ending. Nadeia flew from Zurich back to America.

During the remaining few days Jerom and I spent with Robert before we returned to London, we discussed my future. I told Robert that I did not want to continue with the school of English and would like to study in the School of Acting in Swiss Cottage in London. He was against the idea of my trying to be an actress. I had to give in to his wishes. I casually mentioned hairdressing as a possibility, and he seemed to be agreeable to the idea and encouraged me to take it up.

At the end of the holiday, things were dwindling down the drain as far as our relationship was concerned. When he drove us to the airport in his car, he expressed the view that he was very pessimistic about the longevity of our relationship.

When I got back to London, I left the school of English and enrolled into the school of hairdressing.

I did not see Robert for seven weeks because he went to Asia. I lived like a social hermit for the greater part of those seven weeks. The search for a husband in Switzerland ended in fiasco. I had given up Pranty because I felt no lasting relationship would develop between us, a feeling accentuated by his sexual weakness. I also severed any contacts I had made through the computer dating service in London. I had met several men through it and did not give them enough time to know me, because, after spending an evening in a restaurant or over a drink, I thought they were incompatible with me. To my faults and to my stupidity, I become too choosy.

I had the occasion to meet a professor of law through the agency. He capitulated when I made a mistake and told him I had a boyfriend who was a millionaire. He told me nobody could compete with a millionaire. Although I mentioned him to Robert, I did not mention the fact that the professor thought no one could compete with him. That would have given him a big-headed ego.

When Robert returned from Asia, he brought me diamond earrings, which he said he bought in a factory in Thailand. They were quite cheap in Thailand, but that did not detract from their value or my appreciation of them.

The present seemed to bring together what was becoming a very tatty relationship. After that, things seemed to go on smoothly for a while, until I got a telephone call from him after 1:00 a.m. one night when he said he had a dream he would like to discuss with me. Narrating the details of the so-called dream, he gave me a blow-by-blow description of what Pranty looked like. He also said in the dream this lover-boy of mine traveled all the way from Switzerland to see me in London. Moreover, to add insult to injury, I had the guts to take him around London in a car he bought for me.

I was flabbergasted. As a subterfuge, I replied by saying I had severed all contacts I made through the computer dating service, and I had been very occupied with the school of hairdressing, which took my time from 9:00 a.m. to 5:00 p.m. By the time I got home in the evening, I was too shattered to have any time to socialize.

This, incidentally, was what happened while he was in Asia. There was of course the odd outing to a disco with an Israeli girl who was a friend of mine. Most of the boys we met in the disco were too young for me anyway.

He did not believe my side of the story. When he eventually dropped the telephone, I broke out in a cold sweat. I was convinced he had hired a detective to watch my activities. The next evening, he telephoned again on the same subject. I accused him of spying on me, and that he had no right to do that. He said he did hire a detective, but afterwards, he denied it when I expressed anger at the idea. However, he refused to disclose the source of his information.

Three weeks later, when he came to London, I met him at the airport, and almost immediately, he started interrogating me, wanting to know the identity of the man I had gone out with. Though my behavior implied that I had really gone out with the man in his so-called dream, I did not admit it in words. I was too frightened to divulge any information to him, because, with his influence in Nidau, he could easily destroy Pranty's career if he could not contain his anger. When I drove him back to the airport, he was still demanding to know the identity of the man.

Arguments about him raged over the phone for another fortnight until Robert came to spend another weekend. He became so obsessed with finding the man that he jumped to the conclusion that it had to be a fruitier whose fruit shop was not too far away from his factory in Biene.

Because of his relentless pressure on me, I was beginning to be paranoid about the whole affair. I promised I would tell him who the man was only if he disclosed the source of his information to me. He told me Lenna had told him, and her exact words were, "I have never seen Ruthi with other men before. I was surprised a young man came all the way from Switzerland to see her, and we all went to a wimpy bar together."

I felt a mixture of hatred and surprise. Hatred because I did not expect Lenna to be so spiteful as to tell Robert such a thing, knowing full well that it could lead to a separation between Robert and I. Surprise because I thought she was my friend.

I was curios to know what Lenna was doing in Switzerland while I was not there, and when she told him. Apparently, she was arrested at the airport by the Swiss police because she had checked herself out illegally from a hotel, leaving an enormous unpaid bill behind. When she came on another visit, the police apprehended her. She telephoned him for help, and he had paid the bill to stop the police from throwing her in jail. In a fit of rage, I told him Lenna would never go to bed with him if that was why he did it. He gave me a mocking laugh, and said, apart from the fact that she was too young for him, she was too skinny and unattractive. And otherwise, she was at his mercy and would have done it very easily if he had wanted to.

I kept my bargain, and as the honest and naive person that I was, I told him the name of the man whom I had gone out with was Pranty. Perhaps in a bid to tell me he was not without female admirers, he said there was a woman who was crazy about him. I laughed at him and said if he expected me to believe that, at the age of sixty, a woman would be crazy about him, he had another thing coming. He said if he told me the details, our relationship would probably go down. I was very curious to know who his admirer was, so I pretended I did not believe he was telling me the truth.

In order to prove the truth of his story, he went to the wardrobe and brought out a letter which he handed over to me to read. It was a love letter written by a woman in the Philippines. Having gone through it, I said it probably came from one of the prostitutes he met on his tour of Asia to which he quickly cut in and said he had met her when he was buying cigars in a shop. She was an innocent girl whom he later had a very interesting discussion with when he invited her for a walk.

I told him I must be a sharp contrast from her. She was everything I was not. She must have been innocent and probably as beautiful as a goddess. I said, whereas he had met me as a hostess in a club, his lady admirer in the Philippines sold cigarettes, and that made the difference between a bad woman and a good woman. Since I did not feel competent enough to fight with her for his affections, I would gladly withdraw from the scene.

He later changed his story and said he had met her in a bar where she forced herself on him. I asked him how much the pleasure cost him. He replied by saying her standard of living was very pitiful. She lived in abject poverty in an undignified hut, without tap water, or any modern convenience. He felt so sorry for her that he bought her a stove and gave her a little cash present. She had written about eighteen letters, most of which were affectionate letters, in which she expressed her liking for him. Out of his freewill, he sent her some money.

I said if he was supporting two women in his life, then all the talks about waiting for the right moment to get his divorce were nothing but lies. He made the excuse that she was too far away to mean much to him. I reminded him that all it would take to bridge that distance was for him to send a flight ticket to her to join him in Switzerland.

I blew the whole incident up by saying what his neighbors would think of him if they saw, that at his age, he kept on changing women from different countries. I added, sarcastically, that it would not be long anyway before he reached the end of his tether because youth was not on his side. He asked me to stop talking like that, and that we had both been very stupid by going with someone else, but he felt that we could strengthen our relationship if we adopted the spirit of forgive and forget. I went along with that line of thinking. Therefore, with that optimistic frame of mind, Robert flew back to Switzerland.

CHAPTER THIRTEEN

I

Jerom and I spent the Christmas of 1977 in Switzerland. After our arrival in Nidau, Robert took us to his chalet, which he used as weekend or vacation house for his wife and children. We stayed there until after the New Year celebrations. Throughout our stay there, Robert persisted in his inquiry about what Pranty did for a living, but I continued to suppress the information.

When I was back in London, he had complained to me that I made him terminate his relationship with his woman friend in the Philippines. He wrote a letter saying he was sorry about ending the relationship because he had a woman who deserved his undivided attention.

Two weeks later, Robert came over to London on one of his weekends. He pressed more than ever before on wanting to know where he could find Pranty in Switzerland and what he did for a living.

His continued persistence annoyed me. I reminded him that, before the Christmas holidays, he had promised me that once the festivities were over, he would consult his wife on the issue of their divorce and work out something without having to go to court. According to him, his wife was a Swiss Italian and a staunch Catholic. Catholic beliefs do not allow people to get divorced. His wife was trying to avoid the courts as much as she could.

I said rather than living up to his words and doing something about his divorce, he kept on and on about the identity of Pranty. I confronted him by telling him that perhaps he was too frightened to lose a substantial amount of his fortune if he divorced his wife.

Money was the most important driving force in his life; all other things played second fiddle. He once asked me if I would agree to marry him if he made me sign a contract that if I left him I would not get anything. I told him I would be dehumanizing myself if I signed such a silly piece of paper, but if it would make him happy, I would do it for him.

He put the question before me, that, had I met him a poor man, would our relationship have started at all? Briefly, I was silent because that consideration had never popped itself up in my mind before, so I could not give him an outright and positive answer.

After brooding over it for a while, I told him it was not a fair question to ask. He went on to provide a plausible answer to his question when he said he had dazzled me with his wealth at the beginning of our relationship so that I had grown to

Ruth Toby

love him that way. Maybe if he were poor, he contended, things would have been different.

I tended to go along with that line of thinking because looking at the circumstances that made me go to him in Switzerland, they were motivated by necessity. I was in need, and the only person who seemed capable of helping me at that time was him.

To be truthful, if I had met him a poor man, I probably would never have had anything to do with him.

As events turned out, his weekend visits throughout the months of January and February of 1978 continued to be marked with rows and arguments generated by the questions of the identity of Pranty and what he did for a living. With considerable difficulty and restraint, I kept it a closely guarded secret.

During the Easter vacation, Robert came to London, and we drove to New Forest with the intention of staying in a hotel there, but all the hotels were fully booked. As an alternative, we stayed in a five-star hotel in Bournemouth. Whilst in Bournemouth, argument about Pranty reared its ugly head again, tainting what was a splendid holiday. I forewarned Pranty that Lenna had told Robert about him, and because he was a very jealous man, he should prepare himself for any eventuality. In any event, if Robert would happen to see him, he must never, under any circumstances, tell Robert I went to bed with him, or that we still had any relationship.

In any event, I was not telling Pranty anything new. I was just putting into writing what was already apparent to both of us since we had suspended any form of communication.

I assured him that, under no circumstances, would I disclose his name to Robert, and he could rest assured that unpleasant things would not emanate from it.

Later, in a moment of retrospection, it did occur to me that as long as I kept Pranty's identity a mystery to Robert, there would never be any respite for me. So, one day, I decided I was fed up to the teeth with holding the information from him. I told Robert Pranty was an optician, and he owned a shop in the middle of town. I also told him how I met him and the reasons for his subsequent visit to London to see me.

By telling Robert these things, I managed to remove from my chest a heavy burden that had aggravated me since that fateful night when Robert telephoned me to tell me about his fictitious dream.

However, that relief turned into annoyance, when, a few days after I told Robert those things, he telephoned me to say he took Franswa, our only friend, to see what Pranty looked like, but they were both disappointed to discover how bad my taste in men was. They thought not only did he look like a homosexual, but also he looked stupid and timid.

I protested at his indiscretion of telling Franswa about it and breaking his promise about not causing any embarrassment to Pranty.

When he came to London two weeks later, I told him off about it again. I told him that he had no grounds to complain I had an affair with a man who looked like a homosexual when he himself paid a marriage bureau to look for a husband for me.

I was so angry, I threw the money he had just given to me (he was supporting me financially by giving me 500 pounds per a month) in his face. I told him I was young, beautiful, and very attractive to men, and if I really wanted a man, I could get one very easily without playing games or paying a marriage bureau.

I reminded him that during the last summer, he had expressed pessimism over the longevity of our relationship. So what was he getting uptight about, when, after being with him for five years, he could not make a decision whether he wanted to marry me or not?

He argued with me that I had only lived with him for one and a half years, which was the time we spent together in Switzerland. I told him our relationship had gone on for five years, because, after I left Switzerland, he telephoned me every two days and came over to London to see me every two or three weeks. Not to mention the fact that we were going on holidays together, besides taking Jerom with me to Switzerland.

Throughout those five years, he monopolized me. I was his exclusive property. He gave me orders about not having friends and influenced my choice of a career. I called that living together because I was literally his puppet whom he maneuvered with wire strings.

I told him I was not going to waste my entire life waiting for him to make up his mind on what to do. I wanted someone simple, who may not be rich, but who would love me enough to want to marry me. He kept saying he was a simple man, but I think my meaning of simple was lost on him.

II

At the end of April of 1978, an English woman by the name of Mary wanted to rent a room in my apartment. She was about forty years old, and I thought subletting her room would be okay, since she was older than I was, and her approach to life would be that of an adult. Besides, she would be a kind of companion in the apartment, especially when Robert was not around. A few weeks after she moved in, she broke, as it were, all the rules in the book. She had very late telephone calls from a boyfriend who was a cab driver; her husband came to the apartment to disturb the peace saying Mary should return to their matrimonial home because she had five children to take care of.

She also had another boyfriend who was a married man who frequented the apartment at unsocial hours and had a wife who frequently went to Mary's place of work to cause trouble.

In the early evenings, when Jerom and I watched television in the living room, we used to hear her loud ecstatic cries as she made love. Even the neighbors living downstairs complained about it, saying it was not fair on my young son. I talked to her like a friend and asked her to try to minimize the times her boyfriend spent the night in her room. She complained that if Robert could stay the night when he came from Switzerland, she saw no reason why her boyfriend could not do the same.

I told Robert about the problems she was giving me, and he advised me to tell her that if she would not comply with the rules and regulations every tenant was familiar with, she would have to leave.

III

Robert paid me two visits in May. During the second visit, we went to a place called Cheddar Gorge, which incidentally, Mary had recommended to us in one of our good times with her.

Throughout our weekend, I thought he behaved very strangely. The Pranty affair must have taken its toll on him. He had become a ghost of his real self. Not only was he very cold, but he seemed to be lost in himself. In my mind, I decided I was going to leave him because he had become obsessed with the Pranty affair. The last night he spent with me before he went back to Switzerland was one I will never forget. I made love to him to please him, during the course of which, I experienced a very strange feeling inside me. I felt as if there were pimple-like outgrowths on his sexual organ. I was very uncomfortable. Before he departed, he asked me where I would like to go for the summer, and I told him I would like to go to Israel.

A week later, he telephoned and told me unexpectedly that he had a new girlfriend in South America. She was thirty-three years old. She had put an advert in a magazine about wanting a man between 35-45 for friendship and possible marriage.

Though he was much older than she wanted, they both exchanged photographs and he thought she liked him very much, in spite of the age difference.

I was shocked and said I was not ready to compete with her for a married man. The game was not worth the candle. I also said I did not think I would like to go to Israel on our proposed holiday because I would spoil his fun by being with him because his heart would be with his new girlfriend in South America. I told him to go to South America for his summer holidays.

He replied by saying why not? I felt as if a knife had been cut through my heart, but I managed to bear the feeling. I told him that he might go all the way to South America to find out that she may not even go to bed with him. He said it would not bother him a bit, if anything, it would make him respect her more.

I wished him good luck and dropped the phone while he was still holding the line. He tried to call me back immediately, but I refused to pick up the receiver. When I eventually did, he said nobody had ever dropped a telephone on him before, and I should not do it again.

He asked me, again, if I had reconsidered my decision not to go to Israel with him. I said I still stood by my decision not to go. I also said if things did not work out between him and the South American girl, I would have him back, but if it worked out, her gain would be my loss.

The next day, I wrote a twenty-three page letter to him summarizing our whole relationship. I expressed the view that I was tired of his false promises of marriage. The letter was a kind of goodbye letter to him. I posted the letter the next day. In the meantime, before he got the letter, he used to call me, but I did not want to talk to him.

I told Jerom to tell him that I was out. This happened for several days until Jerom complained that he hated the idea of telling him lies about my not being in. So when Jerom went to bed, I used to remove the receiver from the hook, so that when he called it would sound busy.

On the fourteenth of June, when I knew he must have received my letter, I answered the telephone. He tried to exonerate himself and said he was not as bad as I had portrayed him in my long letter. At the end of his defense, he tried to talk me into going to Israel with him as we had arranged earlier, but I declined again. I told him I had posted the last photograph I had taken with him and that I had cut myself out of it. He said that did not matter much because we could take some more in the future. He apologized for his behavior and asked me to reconsider my decision not to go to Israel and to do the bookings.

I finally agreed to go but told him not to rush things.

He said he was going to call me the next day, confirming when he was going to pay me a visit in London.

I expected his call, but I did not hear from him. I thought something important must have cropped up to prevent him from calling. It was very unlike him not to call when he promised to do so. When I did not hear from him for the next four days, I decided to call his apartment. I called several times until the French woman helper who cleaned the apartment picked up the telephone. She could not tell me anything about him, so I decided to call Robert's office, something I rarely did. Someone answered the telephone in French, and when I asked to speak to Robert, he told me I should hold the line as Robert's older son was in the office, and he would get him to speak with me.

When he came to the telephone, he told me he was sorry to inform me that Robert, his father, passed away few days ago on the fifteenth of June. Although he spoke very good English, I doubted the meaning of the words he was using. I made him repeat himself several times. I kept him on the telephone in order to get more information from him. I could not believe Robert was dead. I was sure the story about his death was his own invention; a shrewd way of getting rid of me so that I would not get in touch with him again.

His elder son sensed that I did not believe his father was dead, and to convince me, he said he had been holidaying in Bangkok when he got a telegram saying he should return home immediately because his father had died of a brain hemorrhage.

I almost went hysterical when I dropped the telephone. I cried my eyes out for hours, pressing my head on the pillow to suppress my loud outbursts. Jerom, who was also crying, tried to comfort me.

Mary walked in with her boyfriend and inquired what the matter was, and I told her Robert was dead. She patted my head a few times in sympathy, and no sooner had she left the room than she burst out in a long protracted laughter as though someone was tickling her.

The next day, because I was not fully convinced Robert was dead, I telephoned his apartment again. This time, Bery, his younger son, answered the telephone. He confirmed that his father was dead and whispered to me that the police were searching the apartment, looking for incriminating tax papers. He said they had already removed all his papers. I could not believe that because I knew Robert was not shady in any sense, he was very straight with his business. The police must have had another reason for going through his apartment. I asked him to tell me the circumstances leading to his death.

The autopsy showed he had died of a heart attack. He said on the day his father died, he had lunch in a coffee house across the street; he met and spoke to an acquaintance who said they swapped a few jokes before Robert left him. He had gone to his apartment, locked himself up, and went to bed, his clothes neatly folded as usual on the chair. What was very unusual was the fact that he never went to bed during his lunch break. The only times when he slept in the afternoon was when he was holidaying in a hot country. His autopsy showed he had died of a heart attack. The next day, when he did not answer his door or make an appearance in the office, they asked the police to break into the house. When the police broke in, they found him dead.

Ruth Toby

Bery also told me that there was a lot of talk around in the town that his father's marriage problems had driven him to commit suicide, but he did not believe his father was that kind of a man; he was a very strong willed man.

What Bery said was quite interesting because it showed his knowledge of his father was limited. In more ways than one, Robert Roberto was a man of strength and character, but he was also a man with a deep sense of weakness. He had told me a few times he felt like falling down the terrace and meeting his death, and how lovely he felt he was. He once told me I was the only person he had. A suggestion I waved off at that time, because of what I saw as an inherent weakness in him, not being able to make a decision about our relationship.

I flew to Zurich and took a train to Biene to see Franswa, our only friend, who kept me informed of everything that happened regarding Robert. I was deeply hurt by the fact that, when I spoke to Robert's elder son on the day he told me about his death, he had said, in no uncertain terms, that he did not want me to be present at Robert's funeral. Obviously, that was for the convenience of his family, because my presence there would show Robert had a mistress. However, I asked Franswa to take me to the cemetery where he was buried; he said he was not buried in a cemetery he was cremated.

For the first time in my life, I bought a bouquet of flowers for someone who had died. Someone who was closer to me than anybody else was in my whole world. He was everything to me a father, a husband, a lover. He saved my life and gave me strength. I began grasp the meaning of dignity. He gave me an education, and the understanding of life itself; he turned me into a real lady as he promised me at the beginning of our relationship. To me, he was everything. Losing him in the way I did broke my heart; that was a very hard shock for me, and it took me years to get over and heal myself.

I also realized that Robert Roberto loved me very much, and many times, I had some doubt about his love. He played too many games with me, not revealing his depths, his real emotions and thoughts to me.

Three weeks after I returned to London, I telephoned Franswa. During course of our conversation, he told me that Robert's two sons had gone on holiday. I was angry and surprised that they went on holiday so soon after their father's death. On second thought, I reckoned they must have had their reasons for doing it.

It was not until Robert's death that I realized how much I really loved him. His death was a great loss to me. Even after two years, it seemed only like yesterday.

Maybe if he were alive today, I would still be fighting to get married to him.

He was the most outstanding man I ever had and probably ever will have. He was a real man.

CHAPTER FOURTEEN

Following the death of Robert, a vacuum was created in my life. One of the most important things he did for me was to build me up to be able to face reality. Our relationship was far from being perfect, but where can one find perfection in this world? Perfection is not the possession of man.

When I was in Israel waiting for Robert to invite me to Switzerland for the first time, his letter of invitation contained the following words: "I will change you and make you a different woman." At that time, what he meant didn't make sense to me. However, in retrospect, I now fully know what he meant by those words. In his own way, he made a lady out of me. He achieved this by providing me with the longest uninterrupted run of stability in my life. I had no moment of want. Perhaps I desired too much by my demands for marriage in my quest to achieve more stability.

Through him, I began to distinguish between propriety and impropriety.

My presence in this world is not a result of my own choice, if it is, I am not conscious of making it. Nevertheless, since I am already in it, I have to cope with life's vicissitudes the only way I know how.

I think the world is like a vast theatre peopled by actors and actresses on the one hand and the audience on the other.

Some people remain actors and actresses all their lives, while others constitute the passive audience.

For the greater part of my life, I was a member of that passive audience, watching a boring play called life; a play that lacked imagination and meaning.

However, I am in the process of leaving that state of passivity. There has always been in me an inclination to leave that state. That inclination has its deep roots in my burning desire to sing.

Singing is one of the most important things in my life. When I sing, I heal my wounds.

Music is my orientation. I believe a song should have melody with feelings that will tell a story. Music is an escape from reality, and the fun of it is that it has its own world. A world that you can swim in and it will make you feel good, especially if you create it. I feel more than ever that music is part of my creation, and I am very strongly part of it.

I am not engaged in the pursuit of excellence. Nature and nurture have not endowed me with the resources for the pursuit of such an accomplishment. However, having lived for thirty-five years, most of which were dull and mechanical, I hope to make something out of a drab existence.

I hope to achieve this through my music. It does not matter to me if I cry, shout, or sing happily, what matters to me is that I must sing. Singing is the fuel that burns inside and keeps me going.

I have deep and sleepy emotions yearning to come out; I must let them out. To this end, my energies will hence and be directed.

THE END